OPRAH
WINFREY

OPRAH WINFREY

Lois P. Nicholson

CHELSEA HOUSE PUBLISHERS
New York   Philadelphia

Chelsea House Publishers
Editorial Director Richard Rennert
Executive Managing Editor Karyn Gullen Browne
Copy Chief Robin James
Picture Editor Adrian G. Allen
Art Director Robert Mitchell
Manufacturing Director Gerald Levine

Black Americans of Achievement
Senior Editor Sean Dolan

Staff for OPRAH WINFREY
Editorial Assistant Annie McDonnell
Assistant Designer John Infantino
Picture Researcher Villette Harris
Cover Illustrator Bradford Brown

3 5 7 9 8 6 4 2

Library of Congress Cataloging-in-Publication Data
Nicholson, Lois, 1949–
    Oprah Winfrey / Lois P. Nicholson.
        p. cm. — (Black Americans of achievement)
    Includes bibliographical references and index.
        ISBN   0-7910-1886-5.
                    0-7910-1915-2 (pbk.)
    1. Winfrey, Oprah—Juvenile literature. 2. Television per-
sonalities—United States—Biography—Juvenile literature. 3. Motion picture actors and actresses—United States—Biography—
Juvenile literature. [1. Winfrey, Oprah. 2. Television personalities.
3. Actors and actresses. 4. Afro-Americans—Biography. 5.
Women—Biography.] I. Title. II. Series.
PN1992.4.W56N53 1994   93-41098
791.43'028'092—dc20   CIP
    [B]   AC

Frontispiece: *While Oprah Winfrey
is an accomplished actress, production magnate, and crusader for children's causes, she is best known as
the award-winning host of America's
most-watched television talk show.*

CONTENTS

—◖◗—

BLACK AMERICANS OF ACHIEVEMENT

HENRY AARON
baseball great

KAREEM ABDUL-JABBAR
basketball great

RALPH ABERNATHY
civil rights leader

ALVIN AILEY
choreographer

MUHAMMAD ALI
heavyweight champion

RICHARD ALLEN
*religious leader and
social activist*

MAYA ANGELOU
author

LOUIS ARMSTRONG
musician

ARTHUR ASHE
tennis great

JOSEPHINE BAKER
entertainer

JAMES BALDWIN
author

BENJAMIN BANNEKER
scientist and mathematician

AMIRI BARAKA
poet and playwright

COUNT BASIE
bandleader and composer

ROMARE BEARDEN
artist

JAMES BECKWOURTH
frontiersman

MARY MCLEOD BETHUNE
educator

JULIAN BOND
civil rights leader and politician

GWENDOLYN BROOKS
poet

JIM BROWN
football great

RALPH BUNCHE
diplomat

STOKELY CARMICHAEL
civil rights leader

**GEORGE WASHINGTON
CARVER**
botanist

RAY CHARLES
musician

CHARLES CHESNUTT
author

JOHN COLTRANE
musician

BILL COSBY
entertainer

PAUL CUFFE
merchant and abolitionist

COUNTEE CULLEN
poet

**BENJAMIN DAVIS, SR., AND
BENJAMIN DAVIS, JR.**
military leaders

SAMMY DAVIS, JR.
entertainer

FATHER DIVINE
religious leader

FREDERICK DOUGLASS
abolitionist editor

CHARLES DREW
physician

W. E. B. DU BOIS
scholar and activist

PAUL LAURENCE DUNBAR
poet

KATHERINE DUNHAM
dancer and choreographer

DUKE ELLINGTON
bandleader and composer

RALPH ELLISON
author

JULIUS ERVING
basketball great

JAMES FARMER
civil rights leader

ELLA FITZGERALD
singer

MARCUS GARVEY
black nationalist leader

JOSH GIBSON
baseball great

DIZZY GILLESPIE
musician

WHOOPI GOLDBERG
entertainer

ALEX HALEY
author

PRINCE HALL
social reformer

MATTHEW HENSON
explorer

CHESTER HIMES
author

BILLIE HOLIDAY
singer

LENA HORNE
entertainer

LANGSTON HUGHES
poet

ZORA NEALE HURSTON
author

JESSE JACKSON
civil rights leader and politician

MICHAEL JACKSON
entertainer

JACK JOHNSON
heavyweight champion

JAMES WELDON JOHNSON
author

MAGIC JOHNSON
basketball great

SCOTT JOPLIN
composer

BARBARA JORDAN
politician

MICHAEL JORDAN
basketball great

CORETTA SCOTT KING
civil rights leader

MARTIN LUTHER KING, JR.
civil rights leader

LEWIS LATIMER
scientist

SPIKE LEE
filmmaker

CARL LEWIS
champion athlete

JOE LOUIS
heavyweight champion

RONALD MCNAIR
astronaut

MALCOLM X
militant black leader

THURGOOD MARSHALL
Supreme Court justice

TONI MORRISON
author

ELIJAH MUHAMMAD
religious leader

EDDIE MURPHY
entertainer

JESSE OWENS
champion athlete

SATCHEL PAIGE
baseball great

CHARLIE PARKER
musician

GORDON PARKS
photographer

ROSA PARKS
civil rights leader

SIDNEY POITIER
actor

ADAM CLAYTON
POWELL, JR.
political leader

COLIN POWELL
military leader

LEONTYNE PRICE
opera singer

A. PHILIP RANDOLPH
labor leader

PAUL ROBESON
singer and actor

JACKIE ROBINSON
baseball great

DIANA ROSS
entertainer

BILL RUSSELL
basketball great

JOHN RUSSWURM
publisher

SOJOURNER TRUTH
antislavery activist

HARRIET TUBMAN
antislavery activist

NAT TURNER
slave revolt leader

DENMARK VESEY
slave revolt leader

ALICE WALKER
author

MADAM C. J. WALKER
entrepreneur

BOOKER T. WASHINGTON
educator and racial spokesman

IDA WELLS-BARNETT
civil rights leader

WALTER WHITE
civil rights leader

OPRAH WINFREY
entertainer

STEVIE WONDER
musician

RICHARD WRIGHT
author

ON
ACHIEVEMENT

Coretta Scott King

Before you begin this book, I hope you will ask yourself what the word *excellence* means to you. I think that it's a question we should all ask, and keep asking as we grow older and change. Because the truest answer to it should never change. When you think of excellence, perhaps you think of success at work; or of becoming wealthy; or meeting the right person, getting married, and having a good family life.

Those important goals are worth striving for, but there is a better way to look at excellence. As Martin Luther King, Jr., said in one of his last sermons, "I want you to be first in love. I want you to be first in moral excellence. I want you to be first in generosity. If you want to be important, wonderful. If you want to be great, wonderful. But recognize that he who is greatest among you shall be your servant."

My husband, Martin Luther King, Jr., knew that the true meaning of achievement is service. When I met him, in 1952, he was already ordained as a Baptist preacher and was working toward a doctoral degree at Boston University. I was studying at the New England Conservatory and dreamed of accomplishments in music. We married a year later, and after I graduated the following year we moved to Montgomery, Alabama. We didn't know it then, but our notions of achievement were about to undergo a dramatic change.

You may have read or heard about what happened next. What began with the boycott of a local bus line grew into a national movement, and by the time he was assassinated in 1968 my husband had fashioned a black movement powerful enough to shatter forever the practice of racial segregation. What you may not have read about is where he got his method for resisting injustice without compromising his religious beliefs.

He adopted the strategy of nonviolence from a man of a different race, who lived in a different country, and even practiced a different religion. The man was Mahatma Gandhi, the great leader of India, who devoted his life to serving humanity in the spirit of love and nonviolence. It was in these principles that Martin discovered his method for social reform. More than anything else, those two principles were the key to his achievements.

This book is about black Americans who served society through the excellence of their achievements. It forms a part of the rich history of black men and women in America—a history of stunning accomplishments in every field of human endeavor, from literature and art to science, industry, education, diplomacy, athletics, jurisprudence, even polar exploration.

Not all of the people in this history had the same ideals, but I think you will find something that all of them had in common. Like Martin Luther King, Jr., they all decided to become "drum majors" and serve humanity. In that principle—whether it was expressed in books, inventions, or song—they found something outside themselves to use as a goal and a guide. Something that showed them a way to serve others, instead of only living for themselves.

Reading the stories of these courageous men and women not only helps us discover the principles that we will use to guide our own lives but also teaches us about our black heritage and about America itself. It is crucial for us to know the heroes and heroines of our history and to realize that the price we paid in our struggle for equality in America was dear. But we must also understand that we have gotten as far as we have partly because America's democratic system and ideals made it possible.

We are still struggling with racism and prejudice. But the great men and women in this series are a tribute to the spirit of our democratic ideals and the system in which they have flourished. And that makes their stories special and worth knowing.

1

TESTIFYING IN
WASHINGTON
❧

ON NOVEMBER 12, 1991, a black woman sat before a packed chamber in a United States Senate hearing room in Washington, D.C., facing the Senate's Judiciary Committee, an all-male, all-white panel of powerful legislators. Just a year earlier, in the fall of 1990, this same panel of influential men had interrogated another black female, Anita Hill, during the highly controversial confirmation hearings on Supreme Court nominee Clarence Thomas. On this occasion, however, the senators were almost reverential in their treatment of the witness before them, television talk-show host Oprah Winfrey. Despite the extremely grim subject of the hearing—the sexual abuse of children—the mood of the panel was extremely positive.

While giving her testimony, Winfrey sat at a table next to her attorney, James Thompson, a former governor of Illinois. She had sought his counsel in April of that year, when she learned of the murder of Angela Mena, a 4-year-old Chicago girl who had been molested, strangled, and then discarded in the waters of Lake Michigan. A 31-year-old man, Michael Howarth, who had twice been convicted for the abduction and rape of children, had confessed to the murder and was awaiting trial.

When Winfrey heard the news of Angela's death, something snapped in the 37-year-old television

11

Senator Joseph Biden of Delaware chaired the Senate Judiciary Committee. Biden had agreed to sponsor Winfrey's proposed legislation.

talk-show queen. "I didn't know the child, never heard her laughter," she said. "But I vowed that night to do something, to take a stand for the children of this country."

Mena's death was just one of several similar tragedies that seemed to mark an epidemic of child abuse in the United States. Winfrey had donated money to child advocacy groups and used her popular talk show as a forum for discussion of child victimization, but she had come to regard such responses as inadequate, given the scope of the problem. So she hired the well-connected Thompson, of Chicago's prestigious law firm of Winston & Strawn, to assist her in drafting proposed federal legislation that would address the situation. The two then worked together to write legislation that would create a national data bank of offenders convicted of child abuse and other serious crimes.

Next, Winfrey asked Joseph Biden, Democratic senator from Delaware and the chairman of the Senate Judiciary Committee, to sponsor her proposal. While it is unusual for private citizens to draft legislation, Biden was deeply moved by Winfrey's dedication, and he agreed to sponsor the proposed bill. "When millions of people look to you," said Thompson of his famous client, "it empowers you to do more than you ordinarily might. This is a woman with extraordinary commitment." On her part, Winfrey was impressed by Biden's accessibility and desire to help. "He asked for some changes—which we agreed to—and he said, 'We'll have hearings in two weeks,'" Winfrey told a reporter. "I was stunned."

Her testimony marked Winfrey's first such appearance before a panel of legislators. A photograph that appeared in a national magazine showed Winfrey fighting back tears as she testified, but she spoke calmly and assuredly into the microphone, recounting the details surrounding Angela Mena's murder. "I wept for Angela," testified Oprah, "and I wept for us, a society that apparently cares so little about its children that we would allow a man with two previous convictions of kidnapping and rape of children to go free after serving only seven years of a 15-year sentence."

Angela Mena's alleged molester and murderer, Michael Howarth, was a convicted pedophile—an adult who commits sexual acts with children. For years, the prevalence of pedophilia in the United States had been largely ignored because of the repugnance of the crime, the sensitivities of the victim, and because reports by children of sexual abuse were often difficult to verify and thus were frequently

Winfrey arrives in the chambers where the Judiciary Committee is holding its hearings. Renowned for her charitable work, Winfrey has given much money, time, and energy to causes that benefit children.

disbelieved. Moreover, pedophiles rarely fit the stereotypical profile of the "dirty old man" lurking in some alley for his next victim; more often, pedophiles are adults in a position to earn the affection, trust, and obedience of children—parents, teachers, priests, coaches, scoutmasters. Sexual abuse takes place not only within private homes, sometimes, most horribly, within the family unit, but within children's organizations such as scouting or in facilities for delinquent children. "Pedophiles seek employment where they will be in contact with children," Winfrey explained to the Judiciary Committee members.

The legislation that Winfrey proposed would make an FBI-administered data base available to schools and other child-care institutions for the purpose (with their consent) of screening job applicants or present employees. Biden explained that in the states where such legislation existed—California, Florida, Iowa, Minnesota, Texas, and Washington—6,200 job applicants or current employees had been identified as convicted criminals. "This is the best proposal that's come before us," Biden stated. "The idea is simple: that you must do everything you can to detect the convicted criminal before . . . another tragedy takes place."

Establishing a national registry of convicted criminals was only the first item on Winfrey's agenda. "This is just the beginning," she vowed. "What we're asking for in this bill is just a teeny tiny step." Next, she intended to lobby for mandatory sentences for convicted child abusers. "We have to demonstrate that we value our children enough to say that when you hurt a child, this is what happens to you," Winfrey testified. "It's not negotiable."

However, as effective as the proposed bill might prove to be, it still would not act to end the frequent abuse of children within families, for it did not create a mechanism for the detection of the sexual abuse of children within the home. "You lose your childhood when you've been abused," Winfrey told the senators. "My heart goes out to those children who are abused at home and have no one to turn to."

What some of the senators may not have immediately realized was that Winfrey's passion and commitment on this issue was born of her own childhood experience. Following the hearing, Winfrey held a press conference in which she recounted her own painful legacy as a victim of sexual abuse. She explained that at the age of 9, she had been raped by a 19-year-old male cousin; filled with a child's ignorance, fear, and shame, she told no one of the incident. Though that particular cousin never abused Oprah again, a family friend and a favorite uncle molested her until she was 14.

This aspect of Winfrey's past was hardly news to the many loyal viewers of "The Oprah Winfrey Show," however. On a 1985 program, Winfrey had featured victims of sexual abuse who told of their experiences. Until that point, on the advice of her managers, Winfrey had never disclosed her own sexual abuse to the public, for fear that her own image would be tarnished; as is sadly true of many sexual crimes, the victims of sexual abuse are sometimes held to be somehow responsible for what has happened to them. However, that day, as one of her guests painfully recounted her history of sexual abuse, Winfrey was suddenly overcome with empathy. She flung her arms around the other woman, wept with her, and suddenly decided to tell her own story on the air. Following that famous program, more than 800 viewers called in with stories of their own victimization and to seek referrals to counseling agencies.

Since that program, Winfrey has been candid in discussing the experiences she had kept hidden for so long. When in 1989 an interviewer asked her how she had ever learned to trust a man, Winfrey replied, "Really, the question is, how did I ever learn to trust anybody?"; her wounds had taken years to heal. As is true of many abused children, Winfrey's unexpressed pain and guilt revealed itself in the form of a troubled adolescence, and as a young girl with her mother in Milwaukee, Wisconsin, she engaged in various forms of rebellious behavior, including sexual promiscuity. But at the age of 14, Winfrey had been sent to live with her father and stepmother in Nashville, Tennessee, and in the structured, loving environment Vernon and Zelma Winfrey had provided for her, she had learned to channel her time and talents in positive directions, becoming a model student and taking advantage of various opportunities as they arose. At just 22, she became the co-anchor of an evening news program in Baltimore, Maryland; in just 15 years since, she climbed to the pinnacle of the entertainment world, becoming a phenomenally popular, nationally syndicated talk-show host, a successful actress and producer, and one of the wealthiest entertainers in the world.

But instant success did not mean an immediate healing of the scars from her childhood, for it had taken Winfrey many years to accept that the child is never to blame for instances of sexual abuse. With that acceptance had come a determination to look for a lesson in all of life's adversities. "It teaches you not to let people abuse you," she explained to an interviewer for the *New York Times Magazine* about her childhood experiences, and she had not allowed the problems of her childhood to limit the vision she established for herself. "I always knew I was going to do well in life," Winfrey said, aware that in many ways she was more fortunate than others who had been abused in their childhood. "I always believed that whatever I wanted for myself I could get. . . . I have such stable roots that I understand that all this is relative. None of this defines who I am." ❧

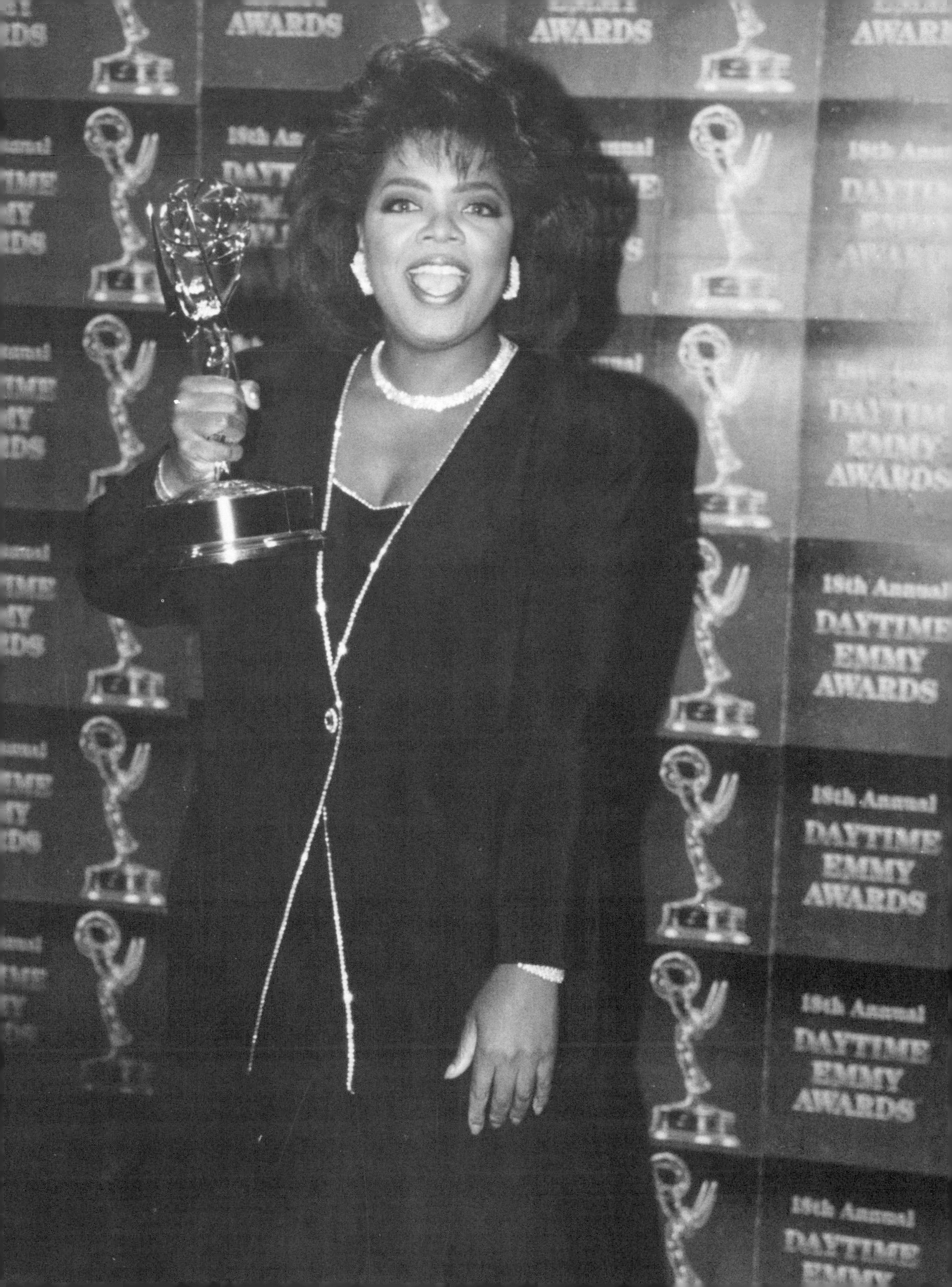
DAYTIME
EMMY
AWARDS

2

A LONELY GIRL

O PRAH GAIL WINFREY was born on January 29, 1954, in the tiny hamlet of Kosciusko, Mississippi, which is some 70 miles north of Jackson, the state capital. Kosciusko was named for Thaddeus Kosciusko, a Polish patriot whose dedication to the cause of liberty inspired him to fight for the independence of the 13 colonies in the American Revolution. A passionate opponent of slavery whom Thomas Jefferson called the "purest son of liberty," Kosciusko left money in his will to buy freedom for slaves from Jefferson's and others' estates. Before Winfrey, the most well-known native of the Mississippi town named after the great Polish freedom fighter was James Meredith, the civil rights activist who first achieved fame in 1962 when his enrollment as the first black student at the formerly segregated University of Mississippi in Oxford provoked rioting that necessitated the intervention of 30,000 federal troops to ensure his safety.

Oprah's parents, Vernon Winfrey and Vernita Lee, never married. Later, Winfrey described her birth as the result of "a one-day fling under an oak tree." Vernon Winfrey lived in Fort Rucker, Mississippi, some 250 miles from Kosciusko; he never knew Lee was pregnant and learned of Oprah's birth only upon receiving a printed birth announcement from Lee on which she had written, "Send clothes!" "What

Winfrey proudly displays the Daytime Emmy award she won in 1991 for Outstanding Talk/Service Show Host. In discussing her career, Winfrey always emphasizes how far she has traveled to reach the pinnacle of success.

19

happened with Oprah's mother and me wasn't right," he later said. "I tell people today that if something like that happens, the boy should help take care of the child."

If the circumstances surrounding Oprah's birth were unusual, the origin of her name was equally so. Lee's sister suggested that the baby girl be named for the biblical character Orpah from the Book of Ruth in the Old Testament. But Vernita gave birth at home, with the assistance of a midwife, and according to Oprah "the midwife got the letters transposed, and I wound up as Oprah on my birth certificate."

Oprah's first years were spent on the small pig farm her maternal grandparents owned in Kosciusko, where Vernita left her while she went north to look for work. Winfrey remembers those years as a mixture of feelings of isolation, loneliness, wonder, and love. Although she knew that her grandmother, Hattie Mae Lee, loved and cared for her, life on the tiny farm provided little contact with other human beings outside the small circle of the Faith-United Mississippi Baptist Church, to which Mama, as Oprah referred to her grandmother, belonged. Grandparents and granddaughter lived in an old, dilapidated, three-bedroom house with no indoor plumbing. Oprah slept with her grandmother in a huge feather bed. Many years later, while looking at a photograph of herself, Winfrey described the child in the picture as a "nappyhaired little colored girl" sitting in a porch swing. "Isn't it amazing," she said. "I remember thinking what a high porch it was, and it's only from there to there. I remember, every time I jumped off, I thought I had accomplished such a great feat. 'Whooo, I jumped off the porch.'"

While Mama was a firm and loving presence in Oprah's life, her grandfather was a more troublesome figure who terrified the little girl. "I feared him," she recalled many years later. "I remember him always

Winfrey's hometown was named after Thaddeus Kosciusko, the Polish military man whose tactics were instrumental in the Continental army's critical victory at the Battle of Saratoga during the American Revolution.

throwing things at me or trying to shoo me away with his cane. I lived in absolute terror." One night in particular remained vivid in her memory: "One night my grandfather came into our room, and he was looming over the bed and my grandmother was saying to him, 'You got to get back into bed now, come on, get back in the bed.' I thought maybe he was going to kill both of us. I was four. Scared. And she couldn't get him to get back in his room. And there was an old blind man who lived down the road, and I remember my grandmother going out on the porch screaming, 'Henry! Henry!' And when I saw his light going on I knew that we were going to be saved."

Like any child who grows up on a farm, Oprah was responsible for several different daily chores. In addition to emptying the slop jar every morning, she had to draw water from the well for the daily needs of the farm and household, take the farm's few head of cattle to pasture in the morning, and feed the hogs. "The nearest neighbor was the blind man up the road. There weren't other kids," she remembered, "no playmates, no toys except for one corncob doll." In this lonely, isolated setting, the little girl's only friends were the farm's pigs and cows and chickens, to whom she made speeches and confided her hopes and dreams. "I never had a store-bought dress," she said later of those days. "We grew everything we ate. We sold eggs. It was very lonely out there in the country."

The Faith-United Mississippi Baptist Church provided the lonely little girl with her only contact to the outside world. At church, she was expected to read and recite scripture and to act in church pageants; in fact, Oprah Winfrey's first public performance was a talk on the theme of "Jesus Rose on Easter Day" that she gave in an Easter program at the church when she was just three years old. "I was always a very articulate child," Winfrey later said. "By the time I was three I was already talking and reading a lot."

Her skill with the spoken word soon earned Oprah the nickname of the Preacher. "They called it being on the program," Winfrey told a reporter about those early recitations. "At a Sunday School performance—all weekend—they'd say, 'And little Mistress Winfrey is here to do the recitation.' . . . I'd have these little, little patent leather shoes. Oh, very proper." Those long days spent in church with the ceiling fan spinning above her head as she watched wasps build their nests near the fan's whirling blades constitute some of her earliest and most enduring memories.

But if church services represented a welcome respite from the routine of farm life, they did not do much to alleviate Oprah's loneliness. Adults may have found her infantile devotion to be endearing, but her peers did not. Resentful of the dominant role Oprah played in the church, other children mocked and jeered her. "Here comes Miss Jesus," they would say tauntingly, and in Sunday school she was spat upon and ostracized.

Oprah's precociousness extended to secular as well as religious studies. In addition to teaching her to read the scriptures, Mama tutored Oprah in the traditional "three Rs" of reading, writing, and arithmetic. The little girl loved to talk, but the problem was that there was no one to talk to, and she did her lessons in the company of the pigs and chickens. On the few occasions when a visitor came to the farm, Oprah was admonished to "sit in the corner and keep my mouth shut."

In the 1950s, "spare the rod and spoil the child" was still the rule in many households, and frequent whippings were considered an acceptable means of enforcing discipline. Winfrey would later describe the way in which her grandmother raised her as "the classic rural style. She could whip me for days and never get tired. It would be called child abuse now." In such households, it was common practice to require the child to provide his own switch for the whipping, which meant that the child had to go out in the yard and pull off a branch for the distinct purpose of being beaten with it—"the loneliest walk in your life" according to comedian Richard Pryor, who was also subjected to such old-fashioned notions of discipline as a child. "In the middle of the whipping you hear, 'Now shut up, shut up,'" said Winfrey. "You couldn't even cry! You got whipped till you had welts on your back. Unbelievable. I used to get them every

Before Winfrey, James Meredith was perhaps the most famous native of Kosciusko. Meredith's courage in becoming the first black student at the University of Mississippi made him a hero of the civil rights movement. This photo was taken in November 1962 at a press conference where Meredith explained that the presence on campus of federal troops and U.S. marshals, placed there by President John F. Kennedy to maintain peace and protect his safety, made it difficult for him to concentrate on his studies.

day because I was very precocious. I was always getting into trouble and I always thought I could get away with it."

But while Hattie Mae Lee was a very strict disciplinarian, she also provided Oprah with ample love and security. In later years, Winfrey remembered sitting, frightened, on her grandmother's lap during a thunderstorm; her grandmother held her tightly and explained, "God don't mess with His children." It was her grandmother, more than anyone else, Winfrey now says, who was responsible for developing her sense of self. "I am what I am because of my grandmother. My strength. My sense of reasoning. Everything. All of that was set by the time I was six years old. I basically am no different now from what I was when I was six."

However, it took time for young Oprah to develop a sense of pride in herself, and when she was young she dreamed of changing at least one crucial part of her identity: she wanted to be white. "I used to sleep with a clothespin on my nose, and two cotton balls. And I couldn't breathe," Winfrey remembers. "And all I would do is wake up with two clothespin prints on the side of my nose, trying to turn it up. I wanted Shirley Temple curls; that's what I prayed for all the time." She believed that if she were white, she wouldn't get beaten so often. "I never saw little white kids get the whippings," she explained.

When Oprah entered kindergarten, she found the tasks required of her and the other children to be boring and silly. Oprah already knew how to read, so activities such as stringing beads and drawing pictures seemed childish and purposeless to her. So she took it upon herself to write a letter to the teacher, Miss New, saying that she did not belong in kindergarten. To her surprise, Miss New agreed, and Oprah was promoted to the first grade, where she astonished the school personnel with her advanced skills. She was easily the best reader in the class, and she was soon advanced to the third grade, where her abilities better compared to the other students.

At school, Oprah made her first friend, a girl named Glenda Ray. The daughter of a teacher, Glenda lived in a brick house near Oprah's farm. It was in that house that Oprah first discovered real toys and real dolls as well as a real friend.

As Oprah grew older, the responsibility of raising her became too much for her aging grandmother, and Hattie Mae Lee decided that the girl should be reunited with her mother, who was working as a domestic in Milwaukee, Wisconsin, and had given birth to another daughter.

An effigy of Meredith hangs from the window of a dormitory on the Ole Miss campus. Winfrey seems to have had little direct experience of the more noxious manifestations of racism in the South.

In Milwaukee, seven-year-old Oprah felt like an outcast. Her mother earned just $50 a week, which she supplemented with welfare payments, and Oprah could not understand why her mother had sent for her: "She wasn't equipped to take care of me. I was just an extra burden on her."

In the urban north, Oprah discovered a kind of poverty that was much more daunting than the hardscrabble existence she had known on the pig farm. Where once her companions had been cattle and swine and chickens, now she befriended cockroaches. "You could find a whole family of them" in the apartment, she remembered. "So I would name them and put them in a jar and feed them . . . like kids catching lightning bugs. I called them things like Melinda and Sandy."

In Milwaukee, there were many more interesting things for a child to do than there had been in Kosciusko—movies and pizza and candy—but they all required money, of which Oprah (or any of various nicknames to which she answered, such as Opie, Opal, Oopey, Ofra, Ofrey, Opera, or Harpo, which is Oprah spelled backwards) had none. Filled with anger at having once been abandoned by her mother, only then to be snatched from the lonely but comfortable haven of Kosciusko for a life of squalor, Oprah began to steal money from Vernita's purse. "I wanted to have money like all the other kids," she recalled.

Unable to cope with her strong-willed oldest daughter, after just a year Vernita Lee decided to place her in the hands of her father, Vernon Winfrey, who was then living in Nashville, Tennessee. So, in 1962, at the age of eight, Oprah was uprooted once more, this time to live with complete strangers: her father and his wife, Zelma. Winfrey had resided in Nashville since his discharge from the military in 1955 and had worked his way from scrubbing pots at

75 cents an hour to a secure position as a maintenance man at Vanderbilt University. A believer in the traditional values of hard work, discipline, respect for elders, and religious faith, he and his wife had established a stable home together.

Zelma Winfrey quickly discovered that for all Oprah's advanced reading skills, she still did not know her multiplication tables, and she devoted her entire summer to teaching her stepchild multiplication so that she would be ready for classes in the fall. Such practicality and dedication was typical of the woman, Winfrey later recalled. "Zelma was real tough, a very strong disciplinarian, and I owe a lot to her because it was like military school there."

Religious devotion was as important to Vernon and Zelma Winfrey as it had been to Hattie Mae Lee, and Oprah continued to be something of a child preacher, speaking often in her father's church and at church-related functions. "From the time I was 8 years old," Winfrey has said, "I was a champion speaker. I spoke for every women's group, banquet, church function—I did the circuit. Anybody needed anybody to speak anything, they'd call on me." She often recited the famous poem "Invictus" by William Ernest Henley:

> Out of the night that covers me,
> Black as the Pit from pole to pole,
> I thank whatever gods may be,
> For my unconquerable soul.

Oprah was greatly influenced by the emotional sermons she heard delivered within the walls of Nashville's Faith-United Church. "I wanted to be a missionary," she said. "I was a missionary for Costa Rica, let me tell you. I used to collect money on the playground every single day of the year. I was a maniac." Just as her formative church experiences in Mississippi had inspired her to become an effective

Diana Ross (center), the lead singer of the glamorous Motown group the Supremes, was one of the first adults to inspire Winfrey with a sense of pride in her race and heritage. For the young Winfrey, Ross epitomized a world of glamour, riches, and achievement far beyond her own straitened circumstances.

communicator, Oprah's continuing experience within the church increased her self-sufficiency. When a group of school children threatened to beat her up on the playground one day, Oprah talked her way out of it by telling the children how Jesus had taken up for the sinner who was about to be stoned.

Oprah completed the fourth grade in Nashville, and during that year she met the woman who became her favorite teacher, Mary Dunkin. After running home from school on the first day of the fourth grade, Oprah excitedly reported to her father that she had the best teacher that anybody could have. She later recalled, "There was always one teacher who stuck out as your favorite, be it the teacher who made you work the hardest, the one who gave you all the breaks, or maybe the one who just brought out the best in you," and for Oprah that teacher was Mary Dunkin. For many years afterward, Oprah wanted to be a fourth grade teacher just like the woman who, to this day, she refers to as Mrs. Dunkin.

Oprah was just beginning to adjust to her new life in Nashville when her mother announced that she was marrying and she wished her to come to Milwaukee for the summer. Her new husband was the father of her third child, a son. So, in 1963, at the age of nine, Oprah reluctantly went back to Milwaukee. Dreadfully unhappy, she survived on the hope that her father would return for her as agreed before school resumed in September and take her back to Nashville. But when Vernon Winfrey came for Oprah, her mother announced that she wanted her oldest daughter to remain with her, responding to his objections with the assertion that since they had never married, he had no legal right to his daughter. "We had brought her out of that atmosphere, out of a house into a home, so I knew it was not good for her, being in that environment again," he later recalled, but he was without legal recourse, unwilling to forcibly remove Oprah from her mother's household, and sensitive about making his daughter, who had already been passed around so much, the further object of a custodial tug-of-war. With tears in his eyes, he bid his daughter farewell.

Although she was often unhappy in her mother's home—Lee worked so often that she had little time to spend with any of her children, and Oprah often felt neglected—Winfrey nevertheless credits her mother with instilling within her at an early age a lifelong pride in her appearance. Lee made it her goal to dress the children and herself well even during times when it was financially almost impossible. During all the years in which Lee worked as a maid, she never left the house in her uniform. "My mother was the best-dressed maid ever known to woman," Oprah said. "You know how you see women going to work at the nice white people's houses wearing slacks? My mother would put on high-heel shoes and her suede skirt and 'go steppin.' It was very important for her not to look the part. She'd get her hair done and go to work."

But wearing nice clothes did little to ease Oprah's continued loneliness, and fashionable apparel could not change the color of her skin. "I felt really ugly in this environment because I believed the lighter your complexion, the prettier you were. My new sister was lighter and she got all the attention, and I thought it was because she was the prettiest. I was the smartest, but no one praised me for being smart. I was teased because I was always sitting in the corner reading; people made fun of me for that. And I felt really sad and left out. My books were my only friends."

Neglected and bored, Oprah began to watch television constantly after school. Her favorite programs were "Leave It to Beaver," "I Love Lucy," and "The Andy Griffith Show." Television also provided Winfrey with her first indication that blackness could be glamorous and beautiful, when she saw the Motown diva Diana Ross perform on "The Ed Sullivan Show." Daring to dream, Oprah envisioned herself in such a role; for the first time, she was made aware that fame and fortune were possible for a black woman in America.

But the chaos in her mother's home still threatened to overwhelm her. Friends and family came and went at all hours, and her mother was often out or at work, leaving Oprah and her sisters to fend for themselves. Passed from place to place, Oprah yearned for the safety she saw in such television families as the Cleavers of "Leave It to Beaver," but the security of Vernon and Zelma Winfrey's home in Tennessee seemed far off. Often frightened and alienated, she reacted by striking back, she later explained: "I started acting out my need for attention, my need to be loved."

3

FROM DESPAIR TO HOPE

ONE EVENING IN 1961, Oprah was left in the temporary care of a 19-year-old male cousin in a relative's home. This cousin frequently baby-sat for her, but the nine-year-old fifth grader never felt comfortable in his care. She was expected to share a bed with him in the tiny apartment, and on this night he raped her; at the zoo the next day, he bought her an ice-cream cone and instructed her to tell no one what had transpired between them. Too young to truly understand what had taken place, Oprah instinctively felt that something wrong had occurred and blamed herself for the incident. Although the trip to the zoo and the ice-cream cone were meant to be bribes, Oprah had no intention of revealing what her cousin had done to her. Fearing that she would be blamed, she kept the dark secret hidden within her.

That same year, during recess at school one day, a classmate provided Oprah with a playground lecture about sex, explaining how babies were made. Oprah, in her childhood ignorance, was horrified to learn about conception. She immediately feared that she might be pregnant. "I thought I was pregnant," she later told *People* magazine, "and asked to go to the bathroom so if I had it nobody could see. That for me was terror. Was I going to have it, how would I hide it, all the people would be mad at me, how

Winfrey as a high school student in Nashville, Tennessee. By that time she had found, under the loving but firm hand of her father, a sense of direction and self-esteem that had been missing in her life.

could I keep it in my room without my mother knowing?"

Although this same cousin never molested Oprah again, the sexual abuse did not end with that incident. Routinely left alone by her mother, she was frequently molested by her mother's boyfriend and a trusted uncle. As with the other incident, she blamed herself—a common response on the part of children who are sexually abused. "I know what it is like to lie in bed and know that other person is there, and you are pretending you are asleep, hoping he won't touch you," she said in an interview long afterward; it would be many years before she realized that she was not to blame.

Like many victims of childhood sexual abuse, Oprah remained silent, frightened, and confused. She felt that she must have been doing something to invite the way these adult men treated her, and yet she felt powerless to stop it. Neglected by her mother, she craved attention; the "attention" that she received from these men was the only "love" that Oprah knew.

Fortunately for Oprah, Gene Abrams, a teacher at Lincoln Middle School, took an interest in her. Abrams noticed that Oprah was different from the other students, who often demonstrated little interest in their studies; while students threw spitballs in the cafeteria, Oprah could be found alone in a corner reading a book. Abrams obtained a scholarship for her to attend Nicolet, an exclusive private high school in a wealthy suburb of Milwaukee, 25 miles from her home.

Winfrey was the only black student at Nicolet, but she encountered little direct evidence of racism or hostility; in fact, she later said, "I was the most popular thing there." Eager to appear enlightened on racial issues and sympathetic to the civil rights movement, many of her classmates made clumsy but well-meaning attempts to befriend her, and she was often invited by her fellow students to their upper-middle-class homes. Though some of these encounters, which represented the first real associations Oprah had had with white people, were awkward, even farcical—in an effort to make her feel comfortable, these families would identify Oprah as their "negro friend" and play music by black performers such as Pearl Bailey, introduce her to their black servants as if they expected Oprah to already know them merely because they were also black, and converse with her about black entertainers such as Sammy Davis, Jr., as if she personally knew them— she generally acknowledged the good intentions that inspired them.

The comfortable existence that Oprah visited in the homes of her friends made her own impoverished life in her mother's dismal apartment seem that much more dreary to her, and she grew increasingly angry and hostile toward her mother. Vernita Lee was working long hours just to keep her family financially solvent, but Oprah wanted all the nice things that her school friends bought with their ample allowances. And even more than material objects, Oprah longed for a father and a "normal" family. "I wanted a family like everybody else because I was going to school where kids had mothers and fathers," she said, and she often told her friends made-up stories about her parents. "I told the biggest lies about them because I wanted to be like everybody else," she recalls.

Oprah frequently lied not only to the other students but to her mother as well, and her anger at being what she called an "ugly, poor girl" soon escalated into delinquency. She stole money from her mother's purse, stayed out past her curfew, and,

During the 1960s the universally acknowledged Queen of Soul was vocalist Aretha Franklin, shown here singing the national anthem to open the 1968 Democratic National Convention. Franklin's generosity had a great influence on Winfrey at a particularly difficult time in the young girl's life.

as she put it, "dated everything with pants on." Her creativity also inspired a series of increasingly elaborate ruses designed to thwart her mother's will.

For example, when her mother refused, because of the cost, to buy Oprah a pair of expensive designer eyeglasses that she coveted, Oprah smashed the pair that she had, trashed the apartment, and called the police; when they arrived, she claimed that a burglar had attacked her, and that she was suffering from amnesia. The police took her to the hospital and notified her mother, who immediately rushed to the scene. Oprah, however, pretended not to see her. "All we know is that someone broke into the apartment, hit her over the head, and broke her glasses," the attending physician explained.

"Broke her glasses?" asked Vernita Lee. "Do you mind if I'm alone with the child for a few minutes?"

Lee glared at her daughter and counted to three. "She got to two," according to Oprah, "and I knew she was going to kill me. And so I said, 'It's coming back to me now . . . you're my mother!'" Lee dragged Oprah home, where the problems only continued.

Oprah's next scheme involved the family's new puppy. When the dog proved difficult to housebreak, Lee declared that it had to go, so Oprah staged another robbery scene, designed this time to make it appear as if the dog had foiled the burglary. She even went so far as to toss her mother's jewelry out the window.

The straw that broke the camel's back, however, came when Oprah ran away. Lugging a shopping bag of clothes, Oprah walked Milwaukee's streets until she happened upon a limousine; as she stared at the vehicle, she was astonished to see Aretha Franklin, the famous Queen of Soul, emerge. On an impulse, Oprah approached the famous singer; sobbing, she explained that she had been abandoned and was in need of funds to help her return to her Ohio home.

Feeling sorry for the teenager, Franklin gave her $100, which Oprah used to rent a hotel room for a week. When the money ran out, she telephoned her minister and asked if he would take her home.

Vernita Lee was both relieved at her daughter's safe return and angry with her. At her wit's end, Vernita decided to take Oprah to juvenile hall that night and place her in the custody of the county, but there were no spare beds at the juvenile facility. So mother and daughter returned to their apartment, and Lee immediately placed a call to Vernon Winfrey in Nashville and made arrangements to send Oprah to live with him.

"Growing up, I acted differently when being raised by my mother than being raised with my father," Winfrey later conceded. "I would break curfew. I'd stay out. I'd run the streets. Because I knew I could get away with it." Vernita Lee had raised her daughter by the "do as I say and not as I do" method. Though she forbade her daughter to have anything to do with boys, for example, Oprah observed men freely coming and going from their own apartment. "This happens in a lot of families where there's a single parent," she said. "Mothers say, 'Don't let some man do this. You keep your dress down! You do what I say!' But the child sees the opposite." When Oprah disobeyed her mother, Lee would threaten, "If you come in here late again, I'm gonna break your neck!" But Oprah knew her mother's threats were empty, so she would do whatever she wanted.

During these difficult times, Oprah, who was just 14 years old, became pregnant and gave birth to a premature baby that died soon afterward. Though little else is known about this unfortunate incident, it was shortly thereafter that she was sent to live permanently with her father—a move that transformed her life.

"When my father took me, it changed the course of my life," Oprah later told a reporter. "He saved me. He simply knew what he wanted and expected. He would take nothing less."

Vernon Winfrey had continued to work his way up in Nashville, and he now owned his own barbershop, which he would later expand to include a small grocery store next door. The business and Winfrey's home was in a respectable, close-knit, predominantly black neighborhood where people knew one another and addressed each other by their first names. Not far from his house was the Faith-United Church, where Winfrey served as a deacon and which would soon resume its central place in Oprah's life.

Winfrey never knew about the horrendous experiences that had contributed so much to his daughter's troubles. "I never knew at the time Oprah came to live with me, that [sexual abuse] had happened to her," he reflected after his daughter had made public the story of her childhood trauma. "If we had known, we might have handled her a little more differently . . . knowing what kind of stress she was going through. But you can't always see beyond the mountain." He did know that his daughter needed discipline and love, and that his first task was to teach his daughter about responsible conduct with boys, lest she find herself pregnant again, with a child to raise soon afterward, and with little prospect of completing her education and staying off the welfare rolls.

Winfrey quickly established hard and fast rules and expectations for his daughter. She would be home by 11:00 P.M., stop slathering herself with makeup, store or discard the halter tops and short skirts she brought with her from Milwaukee, and address her father respectfully as "Daddy"—not "Pops."

Oprah thrived on the structure that her father provided. "I was always a child who was in need of discipline," she would tell fellow talk-show host Joan Rivers. Unlike her mother, when Vernon Winfrey gave an instruction, he meant it, and he would make sure that it was carried out. Later in life, Winfrey would credit her father as the individual most responsible for her success: "I have a great father who used to tell me, 'Listen, girl, if I tell you a mosquito can pull a wagon, don't ask me no questions. Just hitch him up.' That's the kind of dad I had, who was a very, very stern disciplinarian. It's because of him, I believe, I am where I am today."

All that her father needed to do was shoot a look at Oprah and she knew he meant business. The Winfreys were not, according to Oprah, an affectionate family: "We weren't a family with a lot of hugs and touching. Nobody ever said, 'I love you.'" But in place of verbal declarations and affection, her father and stepmother provided Oprah with the things she needed the most: caring and guidance.

The two adult Winfreys were united in their belief that a good education was the key to a successful future for Oprah. Vernon Winfrey had not been a particularly good student, but he held fast to the ideal of a better life for his daughter, and he immediately implemented strict guidelines for Oprah's school performance, establishing a study and reading regimen for her. Every two weeks, Zelma Winfrey took Oprah to the library, where she was supposed to select five books, which she was expected to read and submit written reports about to her parents. Through these required readings Oprah was introduced to such major works of African-American literature as Margaret Walker's *Jubilee* and *I Know Why the Caged Bird Sings*, the first volume of Maya Angelou's autobiography. Such works left a lasting impression on Winfrey by awakening her curiosity about the expression of ideas and her rich heritage as a black woman.

Aside from her father, perhaps no individual has been more influential in Winfrey's life than the multitalented Maya Angelou. As a young woman, Winfrey was inspired by Angelou's memoir I Know Why the Caged Bird Sings *to overcome the trauma of the abuse she had suffered while living in her mother's home. Later on, Winfrey and Angelou would become so close that the writer describes the talk-show host as her "spiritual daughter."*

Nothing that she read had a greater influence on Winfrey than *I Know Why the Caged Bird Sings*, in which Angelou, a dancer, singer, actress, civil rights activist and poet, recounts the story of her often painful youth. Like Winfrey, Angelou was a precocious, intelligent, lonely child who spent her earliest years in a small rural town in the South; like Winfrey, she was abandoned by her mother shortly after she was born, and was sexually abused by a close family friend after she was reunited with her mother in the big city. Although Oprah remained silent about the sexual abuse that she endured, Angelou's response had been even more extreme; she did not speak at all for several years. After she emerged from her self-imposed silence and was reunited with her mother, like Winfrey she also became a teenage mother, but in time, after much hardship, she went on to lead a remarkably fulfilling life of relentless creativity.

To Oprah, the parallels between her own life and Angelou's were obvious and inspiring. Oprah saw her own delinquent behavior as a form of bondage, and, like Angelou, she was determined to give herself voice by establishing a vision for herself. This vision was rooted in her belief in her own abilities and strengths and in her capacity to achieve, inspired by a verse from the Old Testament that would remain as one of her favorites: "I press toward the mark . . . of the high calling of God."

4

BEHIND A MICROPHONE

W INFREY WAS ONE of the first black students to attend East High School in Nashville as a result of forced desegregation. (Though segregation in public education was declared unconstitutional by the Supreme Court in *Brown v. Board of Education of Topeka, Kansas* in 1954, the resistance of white citizens delayed the implementation of desegregation in many areas for years and even decades.) When she entered the ninth grade in 1967, racial tensions were still high at the school, but Winfrey worked to build bridges between students of both races. She found it much easier to fit in at East than she had at Nicolet, probably because her background and the economic situation of her family was much less unusual at the Nashville public high school than it had been at the exclusive private school in Milwaukee.

Though pleased with their daughter's social adjustment to her new school, Vernon and Zelma Winfrey were less happy with the grades she brought home on her first report card—mostly Cs. When Vernon Winfrey informed Oprah that such grades were not acceptable, she questioned his exacting standards, explaining that at least she was passing. Cs were alright for an average student, Oprah's father explained, but he knew that she was capable of more. Then he shared his philosophy of life with his still slightly rebellious daughter, in words she never

Sojourner Truth was one of the many heroic African-American women whose life stories inspired Winfrey. Born Isabel Baumfree, a slave, the illiterate Truth became one of America's most famous abolitionists and crusaders for women's rights, renowned for her majestic oratory.

43

As a member of the drama club at East High School, Winfrey sometimes enacted scenes from the life of Harriet Tubman, the former slave, known as the Moses of her people, who led more than 300 blacks out of bondage to freedom via the Underground Railroad. Most of those were brought to Canada because Tubman, in her own words, "wouldn't trust Uncle Sam with my people no longer."

forgot. There were three kinds of people, he explained: those who made things happen, those who
watched things happen, and those who were never
sure what was happening. Oprah soon realized that
the vision she had for herself was to make things
happen in her life.

Another of Vernon's philosophies was posted in
his barber shop:

ATTENTION TEENAGERS. IF YOU ARE TIRED OF
BEING HASSLED BY UNREASONABLE PARENTS, NOW IS
THE TIME FOR ACTION! LEAVE HOME AND PAY YOUR
OWN WAY WHILE YOU STILL KNOW EVERYTHING.

In addition to the required readings, book reports, and memorization of vocabulary words, Oprah's
parents also set study times for her and monitored
what she watched on television. Oprah later la-
mented that the new viewing times mandated by her
parents meant that she had to miss her favorite show,
"Leave It to Beaver." Instead, she began to watch
more news broadcasts, and she was struck by the
poise, confidence, and excellent enunciation that
the newscasters demonstrated. As a result of the
reading and vocabulary study required of her by her
parents, Oprah's own verbal and written skills improved, her grades began to get better, and her
self-esteem climbed. In a very short time Oprah had
become an honor student and was taking part in a
wide range of school activities.

One of her favorite activities was the school's
drama club. Drawing upon her early experiences of
reciting scripture in her grandmother's church in
Kosciusko, Oprah excelled behind the podium and
on the stage. She gave dramatic readings based on
the lives of such black women as Sojourner Truth
and Harriet Tubman. She also gave a dramatic pre-
sentation from Margaret Walker's *Jubilee*.

At the age of 15, Oprah visited California on a
church excursion. She spoke to California church

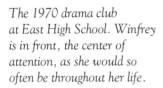

The 1970 drama club at East High School. Winfrey is in front, the center of attention, as she would so often be throughout her life.

groups and visited such popular tourist attractions as Grauman's Chinese Theater's Walk of Stars on Hollywood Boulevard, where the names of famous actors and actresses are inscribed in concrete. Vernon Winfrey remembered his daughter's account of how she ran her fingers over all the names and stars etched in the sidewalk as she declared, "I'm going to put my own star among those stars." Her father recalled, "That was the foreshadowing I had that she would one day be famous. . . . We knew she had great potential. We knew she had a gift and talent to act and speak when she was nine years old. She's never been a backseat person, in school or in church. She always loved the limelight."

Oprah's frequent moves between Kosciusko, Milwaukee, and Nashville had taught her the importance of adapting, making new friends, and getting along with others. At East High School, she soon became a very popular student with both blacks and whites— popular enough to mount a run for president of the student government association. In her campaign, Oprah chose to avoid the racial issues that could be divisive in a newly desegregated high school. Instead, she focused on other matters, such as upgrading the quality of food in the school's cafeteria, improving school spirit, and having live music at the prom. Her campaign slogan was, "Vote for Grand Ole Oprah" (the Grand Ole Opry, country music's most famous showcase, is in Nashville), and she held cafeteria caucuses to discuss the campaign issues. Oprah easily won the election, and her new office provided her with an excellent opportunity to hone her oratorical skills.

When Oprah was 16, she was voted Most Popular Girl in the class. However, her father was quick to remind her that while anyone could be the most popular, it was more important to be the most successful. She dated the Most Popular Boy, Anthony Otey. Like Oprah, Anthony was an honor student. He wished to become a successful artist, was president of the art club, and won medals for his artwork. Anthony and Oprah shared an interest in student activities, and their photograph was published in the newspaper when they walked 16 miles in a March of Dimes Walkathon in which they used the slogan, "Walk a mile for the life of a child."

Serious as they both were, Oprah and Anthony both found time for some innocent romance. Anthony kept a note that Oprah had written to him in Mr. Pate's government class. Dated September 22, 1970, the note was a response, in multicolored Magic Marker, to Anthony's request that she go steady with him. She stated that she could not give Anthony a response while she was in Mr. Pate's class since the environment was too "blah." Displaying her customary diplomacy, Oprah pleaded that she would remember their relationship for a long time and she did not want her decision to be influenced by East High's "blah" hallways.

A true romantic, Anthony saved various mementos from their dates. They went to see James Earl Jones in *The Great White Hope*, munched 50-cent popcorn together while watching Redd Foxx in *Cot-*

ton Comes to Harlem, and cried together through *Love Story*. The two were in the audience for a local performance of the Broadway play *Hair*, which was extremely controversial during the 1970s because it contained nudity and an antiwar theme. One month before Oprah's 17th birthday, they sat in the third row at a Jackson Five concert at the Municipal Auditorium. A month later, Anthony helped Oprah celebrate her birthday at a party held in the school gym, to which the entire student body was invited. That Christmas, Oprah and Anthony exchanged gifts. She gave him one of the wild knit shirts that were the fashion rage at that time, and he presented her with a 40-inch-long stuffed Saint Bernard.

In 1970, Oprah was invited by President Richard Nixon to represent East High School at the White House Conference on Youth held in Estes Park, Colorado. Five hundred business leaders met with youths from all over the country to examine approaches and adopt recommendations on national issues concerning teenagers. For her academic excellence and achievements in community service, Oprah was also selected to represent East High as an Outstanding Teenager of America.

Oprah's star had just begun to blaze. Next she won first place in the Tennessee District of the National Forensic League Tournament for her dramatic reading of Margaret Walker's *Jubilee*. She flew to Palo Alto, California, to compete with students from across the country in the national contest. In June 1970, she won the Tennessee Elks Club Oratorical Contest, receiving a partial scholarship to Tennessee State University.

Oprah had become a very attractive young woman. She was 5'7" and weighed 135 pounds, but it was her poise and confidence that shone through. In 1971, Oprah competed in her first beauty pageant, the Miss Fire Prevention contest, in which she was

East High School was where Winfrey first began to consistently display the poise, intelligence, and ambition for which she has become known.

sponsored by a local black radio station, WVOL. On the morning of the pageant, Oprah just happened to turn on the television as the famous television journalist Barbara Walters appeared on the "Today Show." During the contest, the judges asked Oprah about her future plans. Although she had planned to say that she wanted to become an elementary school teacher, she spontaneously answered, "I believe in truth and I want to perpetuate truth. So I want to be a journalist."

Oprah made it to the final round of three, where the judges asked each contestant what she would do if she had a million dollars. One girl answered that she would purchase material things needed by each member of her family. The next contestant said she would donate her money to the poor. Realizing that the most substantive answers had been given, Oprah decided to go for amusement. "I'd be a spending fool," was her reply, and the judges loved her humor. Oprah later remembered, "I had marvelous poise and talent and could handle any questions, and I would always win in the talent part, which was usually a dramatic reading. I could—I still can—hold my own easily. Ask me anything, and my policy has always been to

Winfrey stands front and center in this 1970 photograph of the East High School branch of the National Forensic League. The purpose of the league, as described in the East High yearbook, is "to develop interest in public speaking and debate, to prepare better citizens in our schools, communities and nations, and to help students develop poise and self-confidence."

be honest, to tell the truth. Don't try to think of something to say. Just say whatever is the truth."

After winning the contest, Oprah said, "I know it's not a biggie, but I was the only black—the first black to win the darned thing." While the contest may not have been a "biggie," it provided Oprah with invaluable experience in thinking on her feet. Before large audiences, beauty pageant contestants are usually asked a variety of questions to measure their poise; these initial experiences were excellent training for Oprah's eventual career. Of the pageant experiences, Winfrey later said, you learn "how to get people to see you the way you want to be seen." Oprah was an attractive young woman with a very nice figure, but she was not a true beauty in the pageant sense; it was her personality that radiated and caused others to like her immediately. Combining this with her desire to win, Oprah excelled.

After winning the Miss Fire Prevention contest, Oprah was invited to drop by the sponsor's offices to collect her prizes: a Longine watch and a digital clock. She was waiting in the lobby when John Heidelberg, one of WVOL's disc jockeys, walked by and, recognizing her, stopped to chat. He was struck by her poise, the quality of her voice, and especially her enunciation. He knew that many people had a negative image of southern blacks, but Oprah's speech had no trace of southern dialect. "Hey, this is a lady who can go places," Heidelberg later remembered thinking. He asked her if she had ever considered a career in broadcasting and then handed her a page of news copy and instructed her to read it. "Sure," she replied.

Like Heidelberg, the employees in the studio were amazed at her poise and her deep, rich, clear voice. Heidelberg taped her reading the news and later shared the cassette with WVOL's station manager, Noble Blackwell. Blackwell was impressed, but other members of the management team were skeptical about hiring a 17-year-old. Heidelberg, however, argued that Oprah should be given an opportunity, and the station offered her a part-time job as a news announcer. She would work after school until 8:30 each school day, reading the news every half hour.

But first Oprah had to persuade her father to allow her to accept the job. Vernon Winfrey had heard that some disc jockeys had a reputation for womanizing, and Heidelberg had to convince him that no one would mistreat or abuse his daughter. Finally, Winfrey was assured that his daughter would be safe at the station and that it would be a wonderful opportunity for her.

WVOL, a black-operated but white-owned station, appealed mainly to black listeners, and it served as a training ground for many young blacks who wanted to break into radio. In the 1970s, on-the-air training was not uncommon, although most radio announcers first attended broadcasting schools. Initially, Oprah worked for no salary while she trained, but soon she was earning $100 a week. Dana Davidson, another WVOL announcer who began with Oprah, was impressed by her self-confidence. "She was aggressive," said Davidson. "Not at all shy. She knew where she was going." Oprah joked that the only reason she accepted the job was that she had nothing to do in the afternoons since she was no longer allowed to watch "Leave It to Beaver." Though she made her share of mistakes—she once left her microphone on while talking to Anthony Otey on the telephone—her work was generally well received.

The radio newscaster was still a high-school student, of course, and as the end of her junior year approached, Oprah served on the prom committee, which was chaired by Anthony. The prom's theme was "Evening Above the Clouds." Blue, silver, and white paper hung suspended from the ceiling while two large white columns marked the entrance to a stairway to the stars. The couple had a memorable evening, dining before the dance on veal scampi at Mario's restaurant and staying out until 3:15 (her father had lifted Oprah's curfew on this special night), but their relationship was nearing an end; different interests and goals would soon move them in different directions.

Oprah continued working at WVOL throughout her senior year. In March 1972, she entered the Miss Black Nashville contest, which was held at the Negro Elks Club and offered as first prize a four-year scholarship to Tennessee State University in Nashville, just seven miles from her home. Though Vernon Winfrey was delighted to think that Oprah could live at home and commute to college, his daughter had different things in mind: she wanted to go away to school, to meet new people and experience new places. Her victory in the Miss Black Nashville contest was therefore a bittersweet triumph for her; though proud to win, grateful for the scholarship, and willing to please her father, Oprah nevertheless regarded attending Tennessee State as a setback in her quest for self-determination.

Oprah graduated from East High School in June 1972. As the winner of the Miss Black Nashville contest, she would be competing against six other contestants in the Miss Black Tennessee pageant to be held later that month in the National Guard Armory in Nashville. When the master of ceremonies called out "Oprah Winfrey" as the winner, everyone, including the victor, was stunned. "I didn't expect to win," she said, "nor did anybody else expect me to. There were all these light-skinned girls—vanillas—and here I was a fudge child—real dark-skinned. And Lord, were they upset, and I was upset for them. Really, I was." She told the other contestants, "Beats me, girls! I'm as shocked as you are. I don't know how I won either."

For much of her life, Oprah believed that it was not desirable to have very dark skin. "I was raised to believe that the lighter your skin, the better you were. I wasn't light-skinned, so I decided to be the best and the smartest." And Oprah was just beginning to realize that being the "best and the smartest" would be her ticket to fame.

5

THE FIRST BIG BREAK

❧

As A RESULT of winning the Miss Black Tennessee pageant, Winfrey was awarded an all-expense-paid trip to Hollywood to compete in the Miss Black America pageant in August 1972. Outwardly, Winfrey gave no hint that anything was wrong, but inwardly she resented the exterior forces that seemed to be dictating the path her life would take. She resented having to attend Tennessee State University, and she did not want to take part in any more beauty pageants.

The civil rights movement had not only drawn attention to the plight of black Americans, it had also illuminated the injustices suffered by all minority groups, including women. The exploitation of women was a subject of increased examination during the 1970s, and beauty pageants were a source of much scrutiny. Feminists argued that pageant contestants were paraded like cattle on runways where they were judged, not on their intellect and abilities, but on their physical attributes. Although Winfrey recognized that such pageants provided benefits for some contestants—in her case, in the form of college scholarships—she shared the viewpoint of many feminists concerning the negative aspects of emphasizing purely physical qualities.

That summer, Winfrey dutifully went along with plans for the pageant in Hollywood. Dr. Janet Burch,

55

a Nashville psychologist, acted as her pageant chaperone, and the two women frequently met to shop for Winfrey's pageant wardrobe. Winfrey selected rather plain attire that made her look older and more career-oriented.

A national pageant was a new level of competition for Winfrey. While she placed less emphasis on personal beauty and focused on poise and talent, the other contestants concentrated on the swimsuit and evening gown segments of the competition. Burch recalled that "Oprah wanted to maximize her talent, her stability, her composure, her ability to answer questions. She completely minimized her physical attraction. That's just very unusual for a person who enters a beauty pageant."

At 18, Winfrey was already experiencing some problems with her weight, but she monitored it very closely and shed some pounds prior to the pageant. "You could see my bones," she remembered. She selected a demure-looking bathing suit that, as Burch observed, "was very, very plain."

Burch's work prevented her from arriving in California until two days after Winfrey had arrived. However, when she landed in Hollywood, the pageant scuttlebutt was that Oprah was a shoo-in, according to Gordon Brown, director of the pageant. Apparently, her manner and poise combined to make such an outstanding impression that she was the favorite contestant.

Winfrey spent most of her time in Hollywood rehearsing for the pageant. Each evening, in a different upscale restaurant, the contestants dined with celebrities; these dinners represented an opportunity to impress the judges. Burch later recalled that "Oprah made good impressions because of the way she was able to handle herself. She did not go off on tangents. She was very goal-oriented."

For the talent portion of the pageant, Winfrey decided to perform a routine that would include a monologue and the singing of the spiritual "Sometimes I Feel Like a Motherless Child." She planned to enter dressed as an old woman with a bandanna wrapped around her head, but her sponsors persuaded her to dress in a black, long-sleeved, long-legged leotard underneath the old-woman clothing, then shed the outer layer during the performance, creating a dramatic contrast.

Meanwhile, Burch persuaded Oprah to wear her hair on top of her head in a more sophisticated style for the pageant. She and the other sponsors convinced Oprah to apply makeup and to wear a colorful gown that revealed her lovely figure. Everyone was confident that Oprah would steal the show.

Winfrey possessed a quality that others immediately responded to. People who came into contact with her at those early stages in her development predicted that she was destined to do great things with her life. "I never questioned for one minute that she could do well," Burch reflected. "I have never seen anybody who wanted to do well as much as Oprah did. She used to talk about things, like how one day she was going to be very, very, very wealthy. The thought always precedes the happening. If you really think you're going to be very wealthy, and very popular, and prominent, and you sincerely believe it, it's going to happen. You see, some people say it, but they don't really believe it. She believed it. People say, 'I'd like to be wealthy.' Oprah said, 'I'm going to be wealthy.' . . . Oprah had a knack. She was bold enough to seek the information she wanted to know. I think a lot of times people are afraid to seek all the information they need in order to move ahead, make a decision, or whatever. Oprah had no qualms about asking anybody for anything."

Saundra Williams of Pennsylvania (center) was crowned the first Miss Black America in 1968. Though such beauty pageants later came under heavy criticism by feminists, the Miss Black America contest was initially viewed as a manifestation of the black pride movement of the late 1960s.

On the night of the pageant, everyone eagerly awaited Winfrey's entrance. When the parade of contestants began, Burch and her other sponsors were stunned: Winfrey was not wearing the gown they had agreed upon. She appeared to be in her high school prom gown, full of frills and ruffles, and it made her look like a high-school girl. Her hair was down around her shoulders, and her makeup was very subdued. Her appearance would have been acceptable in Nashville, but this was a national competition in which contestants were expected to be extremely sophisticated.

It was as if Winfrey was finally taking control of her destiny by sabotaging her chances of winning the pageant. When the talent portion of the contest began, she entered the stage dressed as the old woman. With a bandanna covering her head, she performed her monologue before a spellbound audience, but when the accompanist began to play the first few chords of "Sometimes I Feel Like a Motherless Child," she sang the number without changing her costume. Burch and the other sponsors looked on in astonishment.

Finally, in what seemed like an endless evening of surprises, the master of ceremonies announced the finalists, and Winfrey was not among them; as she later put it, "the girl from California who stripped won." The other contestants embraced Miss Black California before many of them collapsed in tears of disappointment backstage. However, once Burch and the other sponsors worked their way through the tearful losers, they discovered a jubilant Winfrey. To their amazement, she was dressed in the colorful gown that she was to have worn during the competition. Relieved that she was now free from the bondage of beauty pageants, she greeted them with a huge grin, never mentioning the competition or why she had changed all their plans. There was no need for words. Her actions had sent a powerful message about her values and her determination to take control of her life.

Vernon Winfrey thanked Burch for looking out for his daughter. When Burch explained what the young woman had done during the pageant, Vernon Winfrey just laughed and said, "That's just the way she is. Oprah makes her own decisions."

Winfrey enrolled as a freshman at Tennessee State University in September 1972 and continued her part-time job as a newscaster at WVOL. Although it displeased her father, she declared a major in speech and drama. Later she would remember, "I hated, hated, hated college." While her distaste for her college experience may be partially attributed to the fact that she was forced to live at home and commute the seven miles to campus, there were

The administration building on the campus of Tennessee State University in Nashville. Winfrey was never truly happy at TSU. The decision to attend the school had been her father's, not her own, and she felt out of step with the prevailing political trends on campus.

other significant reasons why she found those years to be unpleasant.

The 1970s were a tumultuous era in the history of the United States. Though the civil rights movement of the 1950s and 1960s had resulted in legislation and judicial decisions outlawing many of the most objectionable aspects of de jure segregation and discrimination, many de facto abuses continued to exist, and many blacks were left feeling frustrated, alienated, and hostile by the painfully slow pace of meaningful social change. One manifestation was an outcry for black pride; while the most mainstream elements of the civil rights movement had sought to achieve genuine integration into American society, many blacks, while continuing to demand equal rights under the Constitution, now sought to distance themselves from white cultural values. Other black Americans opposed this approach. Instead, they sought to build bridges of understanding between all the people of the nation by finding common ground.

On the cutting edge of social change, America's college campuses were the scene of much racial controversy. Tennessee State University, an all-black college, was no exception. After well over a century of institutionalized segregation, both blacks and whites sometimes found it difficult to cope with desegregation. Civil rights legislation guaranteed blacks the right to attend college wherever they chose, but as a result of the black pride movement, many black students still preferred traditional black campuses. In these colleges they found a strong sense of their black heritage and a vital source of support from the commonalities among black students and professors.

Campus life at Tennessee State in 1972 mirrored what was happening across the land at black universities. African studies occupied a new but growing area of the curriculum, and many black students wore clothing that reflected their African heritage; the Afro hairdo was also popular. Political demonstrations were common on campuses. Few students were as aware as Winfrey of their black heritage. The readings that her parents had required had awakened her interest in her heritage as a black woman in America, and she was fiercely proud of that lineage. She held a deeply rooted respect for such African-American women as abolitionist Sojourner Truth, civil rights activist Fannie Lou Hamer, and businesswoman Madam C. J. Walker. "I believe those women are a part of my legacy," she later said, "and the bridges that I crossed to get where I am today."

Even so, Winfrey was never a political activist, and her philosophy differed in significant ways from many of her college peers. She agreed with civil rights leader Jesse Jackson, who once said, in Winfrey's paraphrase, that "excellence was the best deterrent to racism and sexism; that the greatest contribution you can make to women's rights, to civil rights, is to be the absolute damnedest best at what you do."

Winfrey's positive experience in predominantly white schools had nurtured her vision of acceptance through achievement. Her successes in oratorical competitions, at the radio station, and in beauty pageants had taught her that she could make it through sheer hard work and belief in her own self-worth. While many of the students at TSU were angry and hostile, Winfrey could not identify with their feelings, and she refused to be a part of something—such as political demonstrations—that she did not believe in. Later in her life, she said of her college years, "Everybody was angry for four years. . . . It was 'in' to be angry. Whenever there was a conversation on race, I was on the other side; maybe I never felt the same kind of repression other black people are exposed to. I've not come up against obvious racism that I know of. I don't think, act, or live my life in racial terms."

Instead, Winfrey preferred to channel her creative energies into being the best at whatever she endeavored to be. For adhering to this philosophy, she paid a price. During her high school years, she had been the Most Popular Girl. Conversely, at TSU she was condemned and criticized by her peers for her unwillingness to participate in their causes.

Just as she had masked her true sentiments about participating in beauty pageants, Winfrey hid many of her feelings from others on campus. Many of her college professors would later be surprised to learn that she was very unhappy during this period, but for the first time in her academic experience, she felt alone and alienated. Her studies suffered, her self-esteem plunged, and she entered into an unhappy relationship with a young man she met, William Taylor.

Winfrey recalled, "My father always said, 'When you fall, you fall so hard.' And it seemed to be true. I'd fall for some guy and it would be life or death." And Winfrey fell for Taylor. She even convinced John Heidelberg to hire him at WVOL, but he did

not last at the station because, as Heidelberg remembered, "He was no Oprah."

Years later, Oprah candidly discussed her relationship with Taylor while addressing an audience of teenage girls. "I have been in the backseat with some Negro with his hand on my breast talking about, 'Baby, you don't have to' in one breath and the next minute talking about 'If you love me you would.' But had I not said no, I could be in a position that never would have allowed me to be able to do the things, be all that I can be, like right now, because when I was seventeen, Lord if William Taylor had've married me, I'd have been married. To a mortician, because that's what he is. I'd be married to a mortician and probably teaching Sunday school in Nashville someplace because I wanted him. Lord, I wanted him. Threw his keys down the toilet. I wanted him. Stood in front of the door and threatened to jump off the

The late 1960s and early 1970s were a time of widespread political protest on college campuses in the United States. In April 1969 at Cornell University in Ithaca, New York, for example, armed black students seized control of the student union building to protest perceived racism on the part of the university administration. Though a scene this dramatic was never played out on the TSU campus, many members of the student body there were vociferous in expressing their dissatisfaction with American society. Winfrey, however, had little sympathy with their views.

Winfrey and civil rights activist and presidential candidate Jesse Jackson embrace in July 1988 at an Atlanta, Georgia, rally. Winfrey had long agreed with Jackson's contention that the best single deterrent to racism is an individual commitment to achievement and excellence.

balcony if he didn't stay. I wanted him. I was on my knees begging him, 'Please don't go, please don't go.' To this day, I thank God he left."

Following Oprah's failed romance, she threw herself into her studies. The late Dr. Thomas E. Poag, the first black to receive master and doctorate degrees in theater arts in the United States, was delighted to have Winfrey as a student. Another professor, Dr. William Cox, who taught at TSU for over 36 years, instructed Winfrey in Theater Practice class. "When she came here she was very much matured. She knew what she wanted and where she was going. I guess that's one of the reasons we got along so well."

Winfrey attended morning classes at the university and worked at the radio station in the afternoon. Still under her father's watchful eye, Winfrey was teased by her fellow TSU students because she only attended classes during the day. When she experienced problems with her car's headlights and could not drive at night, faculty members joked that Vernon Winfrey had removed the fuses from the car.

Despite her busy schedule, Winfrey still found the time to participate in the drama department's projects. When a student wrote a play about Martin Luther King, Jr., Winfrey played the role of Coretta Scott King. She also performed several dramatic readings from Ntozake Shange's *For Colored Girls Who Have Considered Suicide When the Rainbow Is Enuf*, and every Sunday she appeared in area churches, performing dramatic readings from *God's Trombone* by James Weldon Johnson in a one-woman show accompanied by a soon-to-be-famous group called Sweet Honey in the Rock. That same year, she participated in a drama conference at Kennedy-King College in Chicago, where she won second place for her dramatic reading.

The experience in drama that Winfrey gained in college improved her broadcasting skills at WVOL. When a television executive from WTVF, Nashville's CBS affiliate, heard Winfrey on the radio in 1973, he was greatly impressed by the college freshman. Shortly thereafter, WTVF offered her an audition for a position as a television newscaster. ❧

READ

Oprah Winfrey for America's Libraries

ZORA NEALE HURSTON
Their Eyes Were Watching God

6

A TELEVISION CAREER
BEGINS

*Winfrey poses with
Zora Neale Hurston's classic
novel* Their Eyes Were
Watching God *to promote the
American Library Association's
literacy program. Winfrey has
often cited the literary work of
various African-American
women—particularly Angelou,
Hurston, Alice Walker, and
Toni Morrison—as being her
"primary inspiration."*

"WHEN I DID my first audition for my first television job, I was such a nervous wreck, I had no idea what to do or say," Winfrey remembered. "And I thought in my head that maybe I'll just pretend I'm Barbara Walters. I will sit like Barbara Walters, I will hold my head like Barbara. So I crossed my legs at the ankles, and I put my little finger under my chin, and I leaned across the desk, and I pretended to be Barbara Walters." Hearing this story years later, Walters expressed relief that Winfrey had indeed landed the job.

Winfrey may have been portraying Barbara Walters, but it was her own personality that shone through and immediately impressed others. WTVF's news director and anchorperson remembered Oprah's audition: "[Nashville] is a very laid-back market. We look for people who are authoritative in a friendly kind of way, not in a threatening or intimidating way. Not the voice from the mountain, but the next-door neighbor who knows what's going on and can tell you about it. That's what Oprah projected." Harold Crump, WTVF's general manager, made the final decision to hire Winfrey as the weekend news co-anchor and phoned her with the news. Winfrey received word of WTVF's call while she was on her way to biology class, and she immediately headed for Cox's office—she would not say yes until she consulted with her trusted professor. "I need you to help me make a decision," she told Cox. "Should I give up school and radio?"

Cox responded by saying that any young woman in college should be able to think for herself and make a decision without his input. Later, he laughed about Winfrey's version of the conversation. "She swears I gave her a dime to make the call saying she would accept the job. By the way, she never paid back my dime," he chuckled. However, as it turned out, Winfrey did not have to choose between school and television: she was able to both work at WTVF and pursue her college studies. The glamorous anchorwoman lived at home with her parents and still had to obey a curfew.

Winfrey was Nashville's first anchorwoman and the city's first black anchorperson. Teamed with Harry Chapman, her initial task was to learn how to write a news script. The weekend news program did not have a producer, so Winfrey and Chapman decided which stories would lead, how the news would be divided among the two co-anchors, and the sequence of news events reported. They began their work day shortly after noon by consulting the assignment editor. The two co-anchors then often acted as reporters: accompanied by a cameraman, they would cover the news events, return to the studio, write the scripts, and edit the tapes. "Oprah was the kind of person who really got involved," Chapman stated. "She was real close to whatever she was doing and had a lot of sympathy and empathy for those people that she was talking to." However, those very qualities of sympathy and empathy also caused her difficulties as a reporter. "I'd send her out to do a cover story on a family that had just been burned out," recalled her colleague Chris Clark. "She would give them money out of her pocket and cry half the day over this situation. She would take it personally." Winfrey admitted that she found this aspect of the work agonizing, but she stuck it out, realizing that it was a stepping-stone to a better job.

As a result of her years in Milwaukee, Winfrey had never developed a southern accent, which proved to be a tremendous benefit to her in the television news business. She also proved to be a natural before the camera. If she mispronounced a word or made a mistake, she laughed at herself. Viewers found her completely relaxed and comfortable. "You really can't afford to be anything else but be yourself, after all," she explained. "Even if people don't like the subject or are not particularly interested in the subject, if you just always remain yourself or are able to tap into whatever it is about yourself that you can allow to be seen on camera, it works so much better."

For the most part, Winfrey was well treated as Nashville's first black TV reporter. She realized that she had been hired because a black was needed to fill the slot; for her, the timing had been just right. "I was a token," she said, "But I was a happy, paid token."

During one of the first stories that she covered, Winfrey was introduced to a shop owner. As she reached out to shake his hand, the man said, "We don't shake hands with niggers down here." "I'll bet the niggers are glad," she retorted.

Soon, Winfrey worked her way up to co-anchor the weeknight news, where she demonstrated a talent for spontaneously altering the script when she felt it appropriate. Her choice of words thus sounded less "canned" and resulted in a more fluid, conversational delivery that viewers found very attractive.

By 1976 enormous changes were taking place for women in the field of TV news. Barbara Walters left

For young women of Winfrey's generation who aspired to careers as television journalists, there was only one role model: Barbara Walters, who made television history in 1976 by becoming the first woman to anchor a national nightly television newscast.

NBC's "Today Show" to accept a position as the first woman co-anchor in national television broadcasting—with ABC, for an unprecedented $1 million. Many local affiliates took ABC's lead, including WJZ-TV, Baltimore's ABC affiliate, whose managers immediately launched a search for a female co-anchor for their evening news.

At 22, Winfrey was growing weary of being under her father's thumb, and she longed to be independent, but she realized that the position at WTVF-TV was a good jumping-off point for a better job. Unbeknownst to her, a Baltimore television executive had been scouting her work for seven months. When WJZ-TV offered her the position of co-anchoring the evening news, she jumped at the opportunity. With a population of almost 790,000, compared to Nashville's 455,000, Baltimore was a much larger market—the tenth largest in the nation, in fact.

Winfrey arrived in Baltimore in June 1976. She was to be WJZ-TV's first female co-anchor in their newly expanded one-hour news program. The station enjoyed an excellent share of Baltimore's viewing market, and it heavily promoted the team of veteran anchor Jerry Turner and the new girl in town. Turner was a Baltimore institution as a news anchor, and the station's executives knew they had a winning combination in Winfrey and Turner; the theme of their promotion was, "What is an Oprah?" Although Winfrey resented the slant of the promotion, she said nothing, regarding the demeaning nature of the advertising campaign as one of the prices to be paid for success.

Winfrey's move to Baltimore represented the first time that she had ever been separated from her family; she found the adjustment very difficult and called home more than once in tears. "It took me a long time to be charmed by Baltimore," she told a reporter. For the first time, Winfrey had no one to set a curfew for her, and she occasionally stayed out until dawn, expecting some magical change to occur in her life. But there was no magic, only a lonely and alienated young woman in a strange city.

However, one very positive thing did happen to Winfrey while in Baltimore. During a blizzard, she invited another WJZ employee, Gayle King Bumpus, to spend the night. The two young women ended up talking until 4 A.M. and eventually became the closest of friends.

But for a long time, the friendship with Bumpus seemed to be the only positive event in Winfrey's life.

Nothing that had worked for her in Nashville seemed to click in Baltimore. Intimidated by being teamed with a local icon, Winfrey suddenly appeared stiff and formal on the air. When she attempted to be spontaneous, she stumbled over words and looked foolish. In an effort to help, the station decided to "fix" Winfrey's numerous "faults." They decided she needed a new look and sent her to have her hairstyle changed. "They sent me to this chichi, pooh-pooh salon," recalled Winfrey. "And in a week I was bald. Just devastated. I had a French perm and it fell out. Every strand. I was left with three little squiggles in the front."

Not only had Winfrey failed to meet WJZ's expectations; she was now bald as well. To make matters worse, she could not find a wig to fit her larger-than-average head. For three months, she had to don scarves to cover her baldness.

The station's next step was to send her to New York to a speech coach, who criticized her affable on-the-air manner as overly friendly and advised that she toughen up her TV persona. The advice left Winfrey more confused than ever: She wanted to be friendly to people, and it was not in her nature to treat them otherwise; moreover, her approachable style had been the secret of her success to that point. Just when Winfrey felt that she was at the end of her rope, a change of management took place at WJZ-TV, and, once again, the course of her career took a positive turn.

A new manager from Cleveland had taken the helm at the station. Among the innovations he had in mind was retooling WJZ-TV's morning talk show so that it could compete with the very popular national talk show "Donahue." He very much wanted Winfrey to play a major role in the program, but she initially resisted. Although in Nashville Winfrey had once filled in for a talk-show host and had loved the experience, she was suspicious about WJZ's motives for moving her out of the co-anchor slot. She felt that being moved to the morning talk show was a demotion and suspected that the move was a way to phase her slowly out at WJZ-TV altogether.

For the new morning show, which was called "People Are Talking," the station's management paired Winfrey with an experienced broadcaster, Baltimore native Richard Sher. She and Sher immediately clicked as cohosts, and there were few of the difficulties that she had experienced with Turner. From the beginning, it was obvious that the pair enjoyed a natural, effortless rapport that easily translated through the airwaves. For the first program, the station chose a popular subject; Winfrey and Sher would play host to the actors from ABC's daytime soap "All My Children." Years later, Winfrey recalled that first show: "I came off the air, and I knew that was what I was supposed to do. It just felt like breathing. It was the most natural process for me."

Viewers and other members of the media agreed. Dick Maurice, entertainment editor of the *Las Vegas Sun*, discussed Winfrey's natural aptitude for the talk-show format: "She had a special quality about her that made her unique. There was this way she had of looking at you, and you felt that, when you were talking to her, the only person she was thinking about was you. It was a look in her eyes. You could see a soul there." "People Are Talking" became a huge hit in Baltimore; it easily overtook "Donahue" in the local market and was eventually syndicated to markets in 12 other cities.

But while Winfrey's professional life skyrocketed, for the next four years her personal life suffered. When her steady boyfriend, television reporter Lloyd Kramer, moved to New York, Winfrey found herself alone. She turned to food as a source of comfort and indulged in monumental eating binges. Characteristically open about her lack of a social life and displaying her usual sense of humor, she told a reporter for the *Baltimore News American*, "People think because I'm in television I have this great social life. Let me tell you, I can count on my fingers the number of dates I've had in the four years I've been in Baltimore, and that includes the ones I paid for."

But what was happening to Winfrey was not funny. Ignoring the advice of friends, she entered into an extremely unhappy relationship with a man who treated her very badly. Feeling that she was worthless without a man, Winfrey put up with his ill treatment and eventually became despondent, missing work for three consecutive days at one point because she did not have the energy to get out of bed. "I was a doormat," she said. Finally, on September 8, 1981, she decided to commit suicide.

Although she would later feel that she had not been serious about actually taking her own life, Winfrey wrote a suicide note to Bumpus. At about 8:30 on a Saturday evening, the 27-year-old successful television cohost composed the note as she lay on the floor sobbing. In her journal she wrote, "I'm so depressed, I want to die." She noted the location of all her important documents and even asked her friend to water her plants.

Even if Winfrey had not been entirely serious about killing herself, the very act of penning a suicide note caused her to realize how far she had sunk. That night represented a turning point in her life. With the recognition that she was allowing herself to be emotionally abused, she vowed to end the destructive relationship. "I realized there was no difference between me and an abused woman who has to go to a shelter, except I could stay home," Winfrey stated. "It was emotional abuse, which happens to women who stay in relationships that do not allow them to be all that they can be. You're not getting knocked around physically, but in terms of your ability to soar, your wings are clipped." Years later, Winfrey reread her journal entries of those dark days in Baltimore. "I wept for the woman I used to be," she told a reporter about the powerful experience of reliving those days. "I will never give my power to another person again."

Winfrey rebounded from this crisis with a re-newed enthusiasm, and she began to think about a career beyond Baltimore. She was invited to make her first appearance on national television as an "under-fiver" (a role with less than five lines) on "All My Children." She appeared in just one scene but nonetheless spent more than $1,200 on three possible outfits for the role. Though paid just $183.75 for her performance, she regarded the money spent as an investment, believing that the national exposure might prove helpful for her future career.

Having spent six years in Baltimore, Winfrey began studying the markets in other cities with an eye to making the right move if an opportunity presented itself. "When you have finished growing in one place or time, you know," she said. "Your soul tells you when it's time to move on."

Her former producer, Debbie DiMaio, had left Baltimore to become the producer of "A.M. Chicago," the Windy City's most popular talk show. Aware that Winfrey was herself interested in moving on, DiMaio contacted her and suggested that she submit an audition reel (a sample of her work) to the program. Doubtful that a black woman would be given a position hosting a morning talk show in so notoriously racist a city, Winfrey demurred. Chicago had just elected its first black mayor, Harold Washington, and the mayoral campaign had been filled with racial strife. What Winfrey did not know was that WLS-TV executives had already had their eye on her.

Though television executives were almost universally skeptical about the ability of Winfrey's new Chicago-based talk show to compete with the well-established Phil Donahue, her fresh approach and ingratiating personality made her an immediate hit with Windy City viewers.

Finally, Winfrey decided to go for the "A.M. Chicago" spot and met with Dennis Swanson, the station's vice-president and general manager. "Well, you know I'm black," Winfrey said. "Yeah, yeah, I'm aware of that. . . . I don't care what color you are. You can be green. All we want to do is win. I'm in the business of winning and I want you to go for it," came Swanson's reply.

Most people were skeptical about Winfrey's ability to compete successfully with talk-show phenomenon Phil Donahue on his own Chicago turf.

"Everybody, with the exception of my best friend, told me it wouldn't work," Winfrey remembered. "They said I was black, female, and overweight. They said Chicago is a racist city." Other prognosticators advised Winfrey that the talk-show format was on its way out.

But Winfrey took the job, and she was determined to be successful. With Baltimore attorney Ron Shapiro acting as her agent, she signed a four-year contract at a reported yearly salary of $200,000, and she set off for the Midwest. "My first day in Chicago was September 4, 1983. I set foot in this city, and just walking down the street, it was like roots, like the motherland. I knew I belonged here."

7

MAKING IT BIG

WINFREY LITERALLY RECEIVED a chilly welcome to the windy city of Chicago. It was December 22, 1983, and the Midwest was experiencing a record-breaking cold snap. "It was 82 degrees below zero," Winfrey exaggerated. "I remember walking down to the corner and gettin' blown down by the wind, and I said, 'Well, this is a sign I'm supposed to go back to the hotel!'"

Anxious about her new job, Winfrey responded in her customary fashion by overeating. After her first two weeks in Chicago, she was horrified to discover that she had gained 20 pounds. By now, her battle with her weight had become a constant struggle. "I'm overweight," she admitted. "People tell me not to lose weight, I might lose my personality. I tell them, 'Honey, it ain't in my thighs.'"

Winfrey knew no one in Chicago, so she spent Christmas Day working in a soup kitchen. However, on New Year's Eve, she provided live coverage of Chicago's State Street celebration, and Chicagoans immediately took her into their hearts. They loved her warm, easy manner; just one month following her debut, the 30-minute "A.M. Chicago" achieved its highest ratings in years. Debbie DiMaio, the show's producer, remembered that "it was like bringing a child to an open schoolroom—you know, the open classroom, where you go crazy? Do whatever you want

With the immense success of "A.M. Chicago" and "The Oprah Winfrey Show," Winfrey became as much a celebrity as any of the famous stars she interviewed on the program. Here, she adjusts her shades as she makes her entrance to the April 1986 wedding of Maria Shriver and Arnold Schwarzenegger.

79

to do? For Oprah it was, 'Here's your chance to do it. Ask any question you've ever wanted to ask. When you want to ask it.'"

Recognizing that Winfrey performed best when she was allowed to just be herself, the "A.M. Chicago" staff gave her free rein. Carefully scripted questions were written for her to ask her guests, but when she spontaneously abandoned them and made her own inquiries, her questions proved much more interesting. She possessed a gift for knowing just when to say the right words, and her guests felt relaxed and comfortable in her presence. One of her first important interviews was with Paul McCartney, once of the Beatles. Winfrey told McCartney that she had worshiped his poster on her bedroom wall as a teenager and then asked, "I wanted to know, all that time were you thinking about me too?" Both the audience and McCartney were instantly charmed.

Although her interviewing technique appeared to be the essence of spontaneity, it was actually the product of much consideration, as Winfrey explained: "I have the ability to be myself in front of the camera, which is a gift. So many other people play television: they sit a certain way, talk a certain way, even if the set falls down. Vulnerability is the key: people appreciate when you can be honest. It lets them feel more comfortable about being themselves."

The "A.M. Chicago" staff decided to center the program around controversial topics and accordingly sought out true-life stories that held emotional appeal for viewers. The program featured experts in various fields as well as guests with real-life experience of whatever topic was being discussed; viewers could phone in and ask questions also. On January 1, 1985, Winfrey's guests were female members of the Ku Klux Klan, and she interviewed the white-robed women as they explained their views on the inferiority of the black race. Many viewers expressed dismay that

*Winfrey in her studio office
following a broadcast.
Staff members attribute much
of the show's success to her
unflagging attention to detail.*

Winfrey could be so calm in the face of such blatant racism, but the host explained. "What you must understand," she said, "is that when the show is over, those people are still going to be Klan girls, and I'm still going to be Oprah. You can only hope to expose racism for what it is." Displaying her innate instinct for coming up with the right line at just the right moment, Winfrey asked the Klanswomen on the air if they would go to lunch with her, and they answered no. "Not even if I pay?" she quipped.

The program occasionally featured celebrities, and Winfrey interviewed a wealth of famous people during those early days in Chicago, including Stevie Wonder, Shirley MacLaine, Billy Dee Williams, Tom Selleck, Christie Brinkley, Dudley Moore, Sally Field, Candice Bergen, and Goldie Hawn. Ironically, the two interviews that were the most difficult for Winfrey were with her inspirations, Barbara Walters and

Maya Angelou. In their presence, she felt completely tongue-tied.

After just seven months, "A.M. Chicago" was expanded to a 60-minute format. At the end of Winfrey's first year, *Newsweek* magazine featured a full-page article about her. She made her first appearance on Johnny Carson's "Tonight Show" on her 31st birthday, January 29, 1985. When she appeared with Joan Rivers on "The Late Show," the two women began a nationally publicized weight loss contest in which Oprah pledged to lose 15 pounds.

This would be the first of many such televised diets for Oprah. The once-frightened little girl from Kosciusko, Mississippi, had blossomed into a personable, multifaceted, confident woman who had captured the attention and love of the nation's television viewers. It was as if destiny was guiding her through a series of opening doors, each one leading her to her dreams. "People say, 'How can you not be oppressed if you were born in Mississippi in 1954,'" Winfrey told an interviewer. "I always excelled. If you're the best, nobody can put you down." In September 1985, her program was renamed "The Oprah Winfrey Show."

During a 1985 visit to Chicago, the legendary musician, arranger, and record producer Quincy Jones turned on the television as he was eating breakfast in his hotel room. He flicked through the channels, stopping when he encountered Winfrey. Jones was mesmerized by the woman he saw on the screen. He had just entered into an agreement with Steven Spielberg to help produce the film version of Alice Walker's powerful novel *The Color Purple*, and he immediately knew that he was looking at the woman who would play the role of one of the film's most important characters, Sofia. Within minutes, Jones was phoning the film's casting firm; one week later

Winfrey was on her way to California to screen test for the role of Sofia.

She could not believe what had taken place. Walker's novel had been published in 1982 to overwhelming critical acclaim, but there was a profound personal reason for Winfrey's identification with the book. The story concerned strong black women whose enduring strength and faith in themselves had led them to overcome abuse at the hands of black men as well as white society. "I opened the first page and I was stunned," remembered Winfrey, who had read the book while she was living in Baltimore. "I couldn't put it down." Like Winfrey, *The Color Purple*'s central character, Celie, had been sexually abused. Winfrey was so moved by the novel that she bought numerous copies to give to her friends. "If you got married, you got a copy. If you had a baby, you got a copy. If you divorced, you got a copy. I thought it was one of the best books I had ever read."

As Winfrey was reading *The Color Purple*, she realized instantly that it would make a classic motion picture, and she was confident that someone would quickly undertake the project. Secretly, she had dreamed of being a part of such an exciting endeavor, but she told no one of her thoughts. As it turned out, the entire sequence of events, like so much of Winfrey's career, seemed as if it had been directed by some unseen force that was looking out for her. The name of Sofia's husband in the novel was Harpo, which is Oprah spelled backward, and Winfrey interpreted that as destiny's signal. Director Steven Spielberg was reportedly "blown away" by Winfrey's screen test; on her part, Winfrey was ecstatic when she learned that she had landed the role of Sofia. She would later describe it as the greatest moment in her life and credited "divine intervention" with getting her the part. "I prayed at night, 'Dear God, find me a way to get into this movie.'" she remembered. "I would have done anything, 'best boy' or 'water girl.'"

The film was shot in North Carolina, and Winfrey arrived feeling a mixture of excitement and apprehension. "For the first time in my life I thought, 'What if I do my best and it's just not good enough?'" The film's cast included Whoopi Goldberg and Danny Glover, and Winfrey was slightly intimidated in the presence of such experienced actors. She told a reporter, "I'm not accustomed to being intimidated, by big stars or anybody. But this time I was not in control."

In several of the film's scenes, Sofia was required to cry. Winfrey learned to sob on demand by allowing the character of Sofia to overtake her— a wrenching, draining experience. In one scene, Sofia launched into an emotional tirade. On that occasion, Winfrey explained, her reaction was genuine and she was not acting. "Steven Spielberg had them (the other actors) call me 'nigger,' but he didn't tell me what he was going to do. I knew this is what it sounds like and this is what it feels like. After that, I left the scene and wept for a long time."

Another memorable scene was shot as the characters sat around the dining room table. Like Maya Angelou's self-imposed silence in *I Know Why the Caged Bird Sings*, the once-spirited Sofia had likewise not spoken since serving a cruel prison sentence. Wracked with anguish, Sofia is seated at the table, where she rocks back and forth in silence. "I remember having sat there for three days of shootings, rocking at the table," Winfrey recalled. "Mine was the last angle to be shot. I had been sitting there watching everybody else. I had a lot of time to think about the years Sofia spent in jail, and how thousands of women and men, all the people who marched in Selma, who were thrown in jail and what those years must have been like." Eventually, Sofia did speak

The celebrated African-American photographer Gordon Parks captured Winfrey in character as Sofia in Steven Spielberg's film adaptation of Alice Walker's acclaimed novel The Color Purple.

once more. Discussing that scene, Winfrey stated, "Sofia finally speaking was a victory for all of us and for me."

For Winfrey, the most powerful and personally meaningful lines spoken by Sofia referred to the abuse that she had suffered throughout her life at the hands of men. "All my life I had to fight. I had to fight my daddy, I had to fight my uncles, I had to fight my brothers. A child ain't safe in a family of mens."

Released in the winter of 1986, *The Color Purple* was an enormous popular success, but it also stirred much controversy. Many critics claimed that the movie unfairly portrayed black men by focusing on the abuse of black women by black males. Responding to those charges, Winfrey said, "If this film is going to raise some issues, I'm tired of hearing about what it's doing to black men. Let's talk about the issues of wife abuse, violence against women, sexual abuse, of children in the home. What the movie did for me, and what the movie is doing for other women who were sexually abused is pointing up that you're not the only one."

Despite its popularity with moviegoers, film critics gave *The Color Purple* mixed reviews. A reviewer for *Commonwealth* magazine wrote, *"The Color Purple* fails to sing; it merely hums the blues." In February, the Academy Awards nominations for 1986 were announced. *The Color Purple* received nominations for 11 Oscars, including Whoopi Goldberg as Best Actress and Margaret Avery and Oprah Winfrey for Best Supporting Actress. Oddly, the film's director, Steven Spielberg, received no nominations. It was the first time in the history of the Oscar awards that a movie's director was snubbed after garnering so many award nominations. Though Anjelica Huston was ultimately chosen as Best Supporting Actress, Winfrey responded with her customary grace and good humor; the dress she wore to the awards ceremony was so tight, she joked, that she doubted she could have stood up and walked to the podium to claim the award anyway.

In the late winter of 1986, Winfrey appeared in the film version of Richard Wright's classic novel, *Native Son.* This time she appeared as the mother of Bigger Thomas, the story's ill-fated protagonist. Winfrey admitted that she based her portrayal on her own mother. In one of the film's most poignant scenes, Winfrey's character reveals her sense of hopelessness over her son's fate: "I did all I know how . . . and if I left anything undone, it's just 'cause I didn't know and 'cause I couldn't see," lines that Winfrey

admitted had special resonance for her when recalling her mother's difficulties with her.

During this period, Winfrey was enjoying ever-increasing success with "The Oprah Winfrey Show." On September 8, 1986, five years to the day after she had penned her suicide note, the program became nationally syndicated, making Winfrey the first black woman to have a nationally syndicated talk show. "The syndication of 'The Oprah Winfrey Show,'" said Stephen W. Palley, chief operating officer of King World, "was a historic success, and a success of greater proportions than we had seen before. The show has huge household ratings and the kind of demographics advertisers like very much." Within six months it was the highest-rated talk show in syndication.

Winfrey's experience with *The Color Purple* made her realize the power that films possessed for

Winfrey presides over the set at a November 9, 1987, taping of her show. With her are her guests from the program that day: relatives of the seven astronauts who had been killed when the Challenger *space shuttle exploded.*

drawing attention to important social issues. "In a society so media controlled, doing good film is one of the best ways to raise consciousness," Winfrey explained. Motivated by such concerns, Winfrey formed HARPO Productions, Inc., and purchased a block-long building in downtown Chicago, which she transformed into a modern $20 million state-of-the-art production studio containing three sound-stages and offices for the entire staff. "The Oprah Winfrey Show" was taped there, as were other productions; Winfrey was the first black woman, and only the third woman in American history (joining Lucille Ball and Mary Pickford), to own such a television studio.

In the summer of 1986, Winfrey purchased an $850,000 high-rise condominium suite on Lake Michigan in one of Chicago's finest neighborhoods. Situated on the 57th floor, it featured a sauna, a wine cellar, a crystal chandelier, and four bathrooms, one of which contained a marble tub and gold dolphin faucets. The white-on-white living room featured white paneled oak walls and floors, white rugs, generous white sofas, and slim white chairs. The light-filled room contained accent pieces of chrome, marble, and white onyx, crystal vases, and an Elizabeth Catlett sculpture, a gift from her friend Bill Cosby. In the hallway hung a framed letter from the South African civil rights leader, Winnie Mandela. It said, "Oprah, You must keep alive! Your mission is sacramental! A nation loves you!"

Winfrey's bedroom suite featured a television screen, and the condo contained a gleaming tiled kitchen. Discussing her ostentatious lifestyle, Winfrey said, "I bought my cousin a mink coat last week. It's hard for me to remember drawing water from the well every morning and playing with corncob dolls."

One reason for her show's continued success was Winfrey's commitment to controversial topics. In

1987, she took the show on location to Forsyth County, Georgia, where blacks had been excluded since 1912, when a white female adolescent was allegedly raped by three blacks who were subsequently lynched. The county of 42,000 had since been the site of black protests and open racial confrontations, and many people would regard "On Remote in Forsyth County" as Winfrey's single finest hour. When asked why she had come, Winfrey replied, "To explore peoples' feelings . . . to ask why." During the program's filming before an all white audience, black protesters, led by the Reverend Hosea Williams, a black activist, picketed outside and charged Winfrey with having "turned all white." Demonstrating supreme grace and composure, Winfrey never flinched when one of the program's participants asked the audience, "How many of you who welcome blacks or niggers would want your son or daughter to marry one?" Likewise, when a guest explained the difference between "blacks" and "niggers" as "Niggers are blacks who make trouble," Winfrey never wavered, secure in her conviction that the mission of her show was not to change behavior, but to present it in its many revealing forms. She maintained confidence in the intelligence and ability of her audience to judge what they were seeing, and, in time, to apply the information in their own lives. "What we are trying to tackle in this one hour is what I think is the root of all the problems in the world—lack of self-esteem. It's what causes war because people who really love themselves don't go out and try to fight other people."

That same year, "The Oprah Winfrey Show" won three Daytime Emmy awards—for Outstanding Talk/Service Program, Outstanding Direction, and Outstanding Host. The next year, Winfrey became the youngest recipient of the International Radio and Television Society's Broadcaster of the Year Award.

Tom Bradley, mayor of Los Angeles, kisses Winfrey at the annual convention of the National Association for the Advancement of Colored People (NAACP). Looking on are Benjamin Hooks, executive director of the NAACP (rear), and Stedman Graham, Winfrey's longtime fiancé (left). Winfrey has been honored several times by the venerable civil rights organization.

In November of that year, she achieved yet another milestone in broadcasting when she became the first woman to own and produce her own talk show. HARPO Productions purchased "The Oprah Winfrey Show" from the ABC network and entered into an agreement with the network guaranteeing that it would carry her program for at least five more years.

Winfrey also achieved another personal goal in 1987. When she left Tennessee State University in 1976 to accept the job with WJZ-TV in Baltimore, she had not completed her senior project, and she had never graduated. During the years that marked her meteoric rise to fortune and fame, she never forgot the fact that she had not earned her degree. Every time she visited her father, he reminded her that without a college diploma, her success was incomplete. In 1986, she reenrolled at TSU and worked with the faculty to plan a project that would satisfy her media course requirement. When TSU informed her that she would receive her diploma during the 1987 commencement exercises, they also invited her to address the graduating class.

A capacity crowd was on hand in the Howard C. Gentry complex on TSU's North Nashville campus as a proud Vernon Winfrey watched his daughter walk across the stage to receive her diploma. "Even though I've done a few things in my life," Winfrey told the audience, "every time I've come home, my father has said, 'You need that degree.' So this is a special day for my dad." With that, Winfrey then announced that she was endowing 10 annual scholarships in her father's name. "Don't complain about what you don't have," she advised the students. "Use what you've got. To do less than your best is a sin. Every single one of us has the power for greatness, because greatness is determined by service—to yourself and to others." Winfrey later followed her words by personally writing to the recipients of her scholarships and reminding some of them that their grades needed improvement. Her message, delivered in words and deed, was clear: being born female, black, and poor need be no obstacle to success if you work hard and dare to dream. ❦

8

A STAR BLAZES

B Y 1988, WINFREY had reached the top ranks of TV talk-show hosts. Her typical work day began at 6:00 A.M. with a workout or a jog around Lake Michigan and did not end until 8:00 P.M. Typically, she drove herself to work in her Jaguar convertible, arriving at the studio with her freshly shampooed hair still dripping. While her producer prepped her for the show, her hair was coiffed and her makeup applied. She then greeted the studio audience, taped two programs, and met with her staff at HARPO for business and planning sessions. Winfrey signed all checks and made the final decisions regarding HARPO's operations. Finally, she could go home and collapse in bed with a good book.

A testament to her will and determination, the November 15, 1988, show became one of Winfrey's most famous. After a well-publicized liquid diet that lasted for months, Winfrey appeared on her program pulling a wagon loaded with 67 pounds of lard to symbolize the weight that she had lost. In size 8 jeans, she was thin and trim for the first time since her college days.

For another memorable 1988 program, Winfrey returned to Atala County, Mississippi, where the road that runs in front of her childhood home was re-named Oprah Winfrey Road. As she cut the ribbon at the dedication ceremony, tears ran down her

By 1993, Winfrey had become a perennial winner at the annual Daytime Emmy awards.

Aside from her love life, no aspect of Winfrey's persona stimulates more conversation among her fans than her weight. In November 1988, she unveiled the results of a liquid diet that enabled her to lose 67 pounds. She regained the weight quickly, however, when she resumed her usual eating habits. By 1994, Winfrey was slim once more, as the result of a rigorous exercise program and a sensible everyday diet.

cheeks and 370 onlookers expressed their approval of this famous native daughter. It had been a great journey from Kosciusko, Mississippi, to Chicago's Magnificent Mile, and Winfrey thanked God daily for guiding her to her destination.

One day in 1988, Winfrey appeared in ABC's executive offices to hand out copies of Gloria Naylor's award-winning novel, *The Women of Brewster Place*. "Look," she said to each network executive as she handed him a copy of the book. "I know you are very wise and perceptive men, and the only reason you have turned down this project is because you haven't read the book. You could not read it and turn it down. I'll be calling on you Tuesday to see who's read it. We're going to have a book report, fellas." As she promised, Winfrey did indeed return—to discover that only one executive had read the novel. Even so, it was a beginning. Her newest dream—to make a movie of *The Women of Brewster Place*—had taken flight.

Before going to ABC, Winfrey had been turned down in her quest by three other networks. She intended to both star in and coproduce the movie, but she had to find a buyer. When ABC agreed to buy it, Oprah immediately set to work. Before leaving for Los Angeles to shoot the film, she taped four weeks of *The Oprah Winfrey Show* in advance.

As part of a cast that sometimes numbered 150, including extras, Winfrey had attracted two of the nation's leading black actresses, Cicely Tyson and Robin Givens, to star in the program. Winfrey herself played the part of Mattie Michael, the maternal sage of the neighborhood, who counseled the often-beleaguered residents of Brewster Place. The two-part television movie met with success by winning its time-period ratings on two consecutive nights when it aired in 1988.

Winfrey was building a telecommunications empire. Quincy Jones and HARPO Productions purchased the rights to Zora Neale Hurston's novel, *Their Eyes Were Watching God*, the story of a black girl's coming of age. HARPO Productions also bought the rights to Toni Morrison's *Beloved*, a novel describing a woman's escape and recovery from slavery, and the rights to Mark Mathabane's memoir of his childhood in South Africa, *Kaffir Boy*. HARPO became the part-owner of three network-affiliated television stations. Winfrey also purchased an interest in a Chicago restaurant, The Eccentric, which featured many of Oprah's favorite foods, such as mashed potatoes with horseradish. She visited the eatery at least three nights a week to make the rounds, shake hands with customers, and chow down. Winfrey laughingly said that she had entered the restaurant business because she "wanted a place to dance."

As a retreat from the hustle and bustle of Chicago's teeming city life, Winfrey purchased a 162-acre Indiana farm where she could take long walks in the woods, do Tai Chi Chuan by the pond, and grow collard greens and some of her favorite vegetables. Winfrey and her golden retriever often escaped the city for quiet weekends on the farm, where she rediscovered the joys of her country childhood. "I've never loved a place the way I love my farm," Winfrey told a reporter. "I grew up in the country, which is why I'm probably so attached to the land. I love it. I love the lay of the land. I love walking the land. And I love knowing that it's my land." An avid reader, Winfrey could curl up in front of her farmhouse fireplace for hours with a novel, a biography, or a book on spirituality.

Winfrey not only worked hard but demanded that her staff members work extremely hard as well. Employees have described her as a perfectionist who demands the same of her staff, but everyone agrees

Winfrey in her role as Mattie Michael, the indomitable matriarch of Brewster Place. Although the television movie Winfrey made of Gloria Naylor's novel The Women of Brewster Place *was a critical and commercial success, the television series that resulted stands as one of her few failures.*

that she is always fair. Few employees have objected to her demanding style, for she is also notoriously generous with both friends and employees. One Christmas, she presented her old friend Gayle King Bumpus with a check for $1,250,000. In 1987, she took her three producers and her publicist to New York for a Christmas shopping spree. After they arrived at the hotel, she sent the four women a note that read, "Bergdorf's or Bloomingdale's—you have 10 minutes to decide."

As if finally able to fulfill fantasies beyond her wildest dreams, Winfrey's treat to her staff had just begun. Christine Tardio, one of Winfrey's producers, recalled, "We go to Bergdorf's and she hands us each an envelope and in the envelope is a slip of paper and it says you have one hour to spend X amount of money. So we are frantically running around shopping and then she walks around and pays for everything." The following morning, the three women awoke to find a piece of paper under their door. It instructed them to decide on boots or shoes. When the boots had been purchased, another note told them to choose leather or lace. And so the day went. "We're being driven around New York, drinking champagne," recalled Tardio. Next, Winfrey blindfolded them and had them walk through a door. When they removed the blindfolds, they discovered themselves to be in a furrier's shop and in possession of another note informing them that they could have anything in the store except sable. The four walked out with coats: three minks and a fox.

Winfrey never forgot her own struggle to reach the top. "My mission is to use this position, power, and money to create opportunities for other people," she has said, and she employs only those who are interested in self-improvement. In return for her dedication to them, she has earned her staff's undying loyalty. "I would take a bullet for her," said her producer Mary Kay Clinton.

Winfrey was also a generous contributor to numerous charities. She established a Little Sisters program in Chicago's Cabrini Green housing projects and devoted two afternoons each month to that cause, counseling the young women not to get pregnant and to stay in school. On her first visit, the girls expected Winfrey to take them to some lavish spot and were somewhat surprised when she took them to the library and got them library cards! On subsequent visits, however, Winfrey entertained them with such activities as movies, shopping sprees, and dining out.

In 1989, Ms. magazine chose Winfrey as their Woman of the Year for "showing women that we can climb as high as we want to go and inspiring us to take control of our resources and make them work for us and for a better world." Maya Angelou wrote a tribute to her, praising the young woman who had sought her out as a mentor. "Oprah, as talk-show host, tries to manage a calm facade as she lends an ear to brutes, bigots, and bagmen, but her face betrays her. Her eyes fill with tears when she listens to the lament of mothers mistreated by their offspring, and they dart indignantly at the report of cruelty against children and savagery against the handicapped. The even, full lips spread into a wide, open smile when a guest or audience member reveals a daring spirit and a benevolent wit."

Despite Winfrey's fabulous wealth and success, she was not immune to the tragedies that sometimes fall upon all families. In 1989, her half brother died of AIDS. And in 1990, her half sister went to the tabloids with the news that Winfrey had been an unwed teenage mother whose premature baby had not survived. Winfrey declared that her sister's disclosure was the most painful thing ever to happen to her. "What was printed was awful enough, but the worst thing for me was the sense of betrayal. It was knowing family had sat in the office of the tabloids to purposely hurt me. It was as bad as it gets. But I kept reminding myself to look for the lesson."

In an interview with Pearl Cleage, appearing in the June 1991 issue of *Essence*, Winfrey said that it took the terrible disclosure of her secret in the tabloids to make her realize that she had been carrying around this burden of guilt since childhood. "I connected my own sexual promiscuity as a teenager with the sexual abuse I had suffered as a child. . . . I know that there are other lessons there for me to learn, but the first one was that I was not responsible for the abuse and that I had to get rid of the shame I was carrying." The ordeal of the tabloid story taught Winfrey a valuable lesson about her faith as well. "It's easy to have faith when everything is wonderful. Real faith is knowing that no matter what, you're going to be all right."

Despite her enormous financial success and her seeming Midas touch, not everything Winfrey handled turned to gold. In 1989, ABC and HARPO agreed to coproduce "Brewster Place" as a weekly show, with Winfrey starring as the matronly Mattie Michael. "I deliberately put on cotton underpants when I played her," said Oprah. "It made me feel like her." However, when "Brewster Place" did poorly in the ratings, it was dropped from production after just 10 airings. The doomed project wound up costing HARPO Productions an estimated $10 million. The ordeal left Winfrey physically and emotionally exhausted, and her $20 million production studio sat largely unused for several years.

But, as always, Winfrey drew a lesson from the experience. "I don't believe in failure," she said. "It is not failure if you enjoyed the process. Does failure mean *Brewster Place* didn't work? People say, 'Oh, she's had that one big failure,' but I don't perceive it as such. I learned from my mistakes on *Brewster Place*. I'm glad I did and I won't make those mistakes again."

By 1990, an estimated 16 million viewers watched "The Oprah Winfrey Show" each day; with an annual income of upwards of $25 million dollars, the show's host had become one of the wealthiest and most powerful women in America. That year, to make her happiness complete, Winfrey met Stedman Graham, a former college basketball player and model who headed a North Carolina–based public relations firm. Winfrey liked to joke that "she prayed and prayed for a good, hard-working man, and 'Lord, let him be tall'"; Graham was six-foot six.

As a celebrity, Winfrey was naturally the focus of much media attention. Her picture graced the covers of leading magazines, and the tabloids routinely reported on every imaginable aspect of her life, focusing frequently on her weight and the fact that she had regained the highly publicized lost 67 pounds.

Permanently engaged? Winfrey with Stedman Graham, the public relations man to whom she has now been betrothed for several years. The couple persistently fends off all questions about a future wedding.

Another frequent subject of speculation was her love life, especially her relationship with Graham and whether they would be married. "Oprah and I love each other very much," was what he had to say on the subject. "We don't want to succumb to the pressures of the public by getting married, so we are getting married when we are getting married, and not before."

At 37, Winfrey demonstrated increasing confidence, maturity, and sophistication. She openly discussed her evolving spiritual beliefs on her show, referring to her television program as her "ministry." "I am guided by a higher calling," she said. "It's not so much a voice as it is a feeling. If it doesn't feel right to me, I don't do it." In 1989, she told an interviewer, "I am convinced that the difference between how I handle my life and how other people handle theirs is that I don't just pray, I truly heed the response I am given. My friend Maya Angelou told me a while back that she thought one of my greatest assets is my ability to be obedient to the voice of God within me and I think she's right." Winfrey used her program as a forum for discussing her sometimes-contradictory beliefs in a variety of philosophies, including Western and Eastern religions. At times, Winfrey espoused fatalistic theories, such as, "If you were abused as a child, you will abuse someone else as an adult," while at other times she put greater stock in free will. "I was a welfare daughter, just like you. . . . how did you let yourselves become welfare mothers? Why did you choose this? I didn't."

Winfrey's often conflicting beliefs were a critical element in her success as a talk-show host. Her eclectic views enhanced her spontaneity; viewers could not easily predict what her reaction might be on a given topic. They did, however, know that they could always count on her to be honest. At the core of her being, Winfrey believed that nothing that happens in the universe happens at random, that destiny plays a role in all events, and that she was always destined to do great things with her life.

Winfrey's family and friends continued to be a great source of support for her. She had long since made peace with her mother, whom she supported financially. Although her father continued to live in Nashville, the two were "spiritually close," and Vernon Winfrey refused all offers of financial assistance. The only thing he ever asked of Winfrey was tickets to the Mike Tyson–Michael Spinks heavyweight championship fight.

Winfrey obliged, of course; the ability to assist her family financially was something she could easily afford. In 1991 alone, she earned an estimated $40 million, and her financial holdings were estimated at $250 million. She maintained her close friendship with Gayle King Bumpus, who lived and worked as a television reporter in Connecticut, speaking with her on the phone several times each day. She also felt close to her staff at HARPO Productions, and she counted many celebrities, among them Bill Cosby, Quincy Jones, Sidney Poitier, and Maya Angelou, as her close friends. The tightly knit group offered each other much understanding and support, for they understood each other's problems regarding privacy and the demands placed on their time and energy.

In 1992, Winfrey announced her engagement to Stedman Graham in an interview with Bumpus on WFSB-TV in Hartford, Connecticut. "It does scare me a little bit, the whole idea of being married to somebody for the rest of your life," Winfrey told her friend. Despite abundant rumors that the wedding would take place the following year, the couple steadfastly maintained that they were in no hurry to wed, and subsequent events have proved the truth of that particular assertion.

In 1992, *Forbes* magazine, a financial periodical, reported that Bill Cosby and Winfrey were the top two moneymaking celebrities in the world. The publication estimated Winfrey's earnings for the past two years to be $88 million, second only to Cosby's. Winfrey took the role that this wealth afforded her very seriously. She established a foundation to manage the flow of charitable requests that she received, but she did not seek tax-exempt status for the foundation. As Armstrong Williams, the foundation's director, explained, "She wanted the freedom to give money to the many causes she supports that do not have nonprofit tax-exempt status." One of her donations was a personal check for $1 million to Morehouse College, a black college in Atlanta,

Georgia. When August Wilson's play, *The Piano Lesson*, opened on Broadway, Winfrey bought all the tickets to one performance of the show and donated them to A Better Chance, a Boston organization that arranges for minority students to attend leading private schools such as Groton, St. Paul's, Concord, and Thatcher. Winfrey also continues to make several personal appearances a month to speak in support of such causes as battered women and rape victims. To this day, she regards her 1991 testimony before the Senate Judiciary Committee regarding her proposed screening legislation as her single most important public performance. President Clinton signed the bill into law in December 1993.

In 1993 pop star Michael Jackson decided to give his first live, televised interview in 14 years. Wanting to speak only to someone he felt he could trust,

Winfrey's 90-minute interview with pop star Michael Jackson, which aired in February 1993, drew some of the highest ratings of her career. Though just getting Jackson to agree to the interview qualified as something of a broadcasting coup, the interview left many questions about the singer's mysterious personal life unanswered.

Jackson selected Winfrey to conduct the 90-minute interview, which aired on February 10 to an estimated television audience of 90 million. During the revealing interview, Winfrey asked one intriguing question after another about a wide range of topics, enticing Jackson, for example, to speak for the first time publicly about the bizarre transformation of his appearance over the years and the odd personal habits that had led some to regard the reclusive singer as an eccentric or freak. Meanwhile, "The Oprah Winfrey Show" continued its enormous success, winning the 1993 Emmy award for Best Talk Show.

In June 1993, Winfrey attended the American Book Sellers Convention in Miami, Florida, to promote the upcoming publication of her autobiography. "Writing this book has been like 10 years of therapy for me," Winfrey said at an authors' breakfast at the convention. "I'm so excited by it—I wish that I could be on my own show selling this book." Just several days later, however, Winfrey startled the publishing world when she announced she was pulling the book from publication. It would be premature to release her book, Winfrey explained. "I am in the heart of the learning curve," she said. "I feel there are important discoveries yet to be made."

Although Winfrey may have still been "in the heart of the learning curve" there were some things that she knew about herself with absolute certainty. Despite her immense popularity, wealth, and success, she was still fundamentally Oprah—open, honest, and comfortable with herself. Those things had remained unchanged since her formative years. As she told an interviewer, "I still want what I've always wanted. I used to write it in my diaries when I was 15 years old, and I'm still writing it and saying it all the time: 'I just want to be the best person I can be.' That part of me hasn't changed and that's the who of who I am to me."

That dedication led, in November 1993, to what some critics consider her most significant achievement to date: the television movie of Alex Kotlowitz's 1991 bestseller, *There Are No Children Here*, a harrowing nonfiction account of one family's life in Chicago's Henry Horner housing project. HARPO produced the movie, and Winfrey starred, along with Maya Angelou. Although the film was not a ratings blockbuster, it nevertheless constituted an insightful and rare prime-time portrayal of the horrific inner-city conditions—"This ain't nothing but a war field," was how one Horner resident described the projects—that threaten to blight the futures of so many young people in the United States. For Winfrey, the production represented a logical extension of her work thus far and of her well-documented social concerns. "People in the projects are no different from people everywhere," she said. "You can live in the projects and still want a life that's good and meaningful and be hopeful for your children. . . . Everybody wants hope, whether you live in the projects or downtown."

CHRONOLOGY

—————— ❧ ——————

1954   Born on January 29 in Kosciusko, Mississippi

1960   Joins her mother, Vernita Winfrey, and her half sister in Milwaukee, Wisconsin

1968   Oprah's mother sends her to live permanently with her father and stepmother, Vernon and Zelma Winfrey, in Nashville, Tennessee

1971   Becomes first black winner of the Miss Fire Prevention beauty pageant in Nashville; hired to work part-time as a newscaster for a Nashville radio station, WVOL

1972   Wins the Miss Black Nashville beauty pageant and a four-year scholarship to Tennessee State University (TSU); graduates in June from East High School; wins the Miss Black Tennessee pageant and participates in the Miss Black America pageant in August; enters TSU in September

1973   Accepts a part-time job as a weekend news co-anchor at WTVF-TV, a Nashville television station

1976   Accepts a job as the evening news co-anchor at WJZ-TV in Baltimore, Maryland

1977   Named the cohost of WJZ-TV's talk show "People Are Talking"

1983   Accepts an offer to host Chicago's WLS-TV's talk show, "A.M. Chicago"

1985   "A.M. Chicago" becomes "The Oprah Winfrey Show"; Winfrey stars in Steven Spielberg's movie *The Color Purple*

1986   Nominated for an Academy Award as Best Supporting Actress for *The Color Purple*; "The Oprah Winfrey Show" becomes nationally syndicated; Winfrey forms her own production studio, HARPO Productions

1987   Receives her degree from Tennessee State University and endows 10 TSU scholarships in her father's name; "The Oprah Winfrey Show" wins three Daytime Emmy awards; named the youngest recipient of the Broadcaster of the Year Award by the International Radio and Television Society

1988   HARPO Productions produces *The Women of Brewster Place*, a two-part television movie

1991   Winfrey testifies before the U.S. Senate Judiciary Committee to propose a bill providing for a national screening device for employees convicted of sexual abuse crimes against children

1992   Announces her engagement to Stedman Graham

1993   Interviews Michael Jackson in his first televised interview in 14 years; "The Oprah Winfrey Show" wins an Emmy award for the best talk-show program; Winfrey attends the American Book Sellers Convention to promote her autobiography; named a winner of the Horatio Alger Award, given to those who overcome adversity and become leaders in their field

FURTHER READING

Beaton, Margaret. *Oprah Winfrey: TV Talk Show Host.* Chicago: Childrens Press, 1990.

King, Norman. *Everybody Loves Oprah!: Her Remarkable Life.* New York: Morrow, 1988.

Patterson, Lillie. *Oprah Winfrey: Talk Show Host and Actress.* Hillside, NJ: Enslow, 1990.

Saidman, Anne. *Oprah Winfrey: Media Success Story.* Minneapolis: Lerner Publications, 1990.

Waldron, Robert. *Oprah!* New York: St. Martin's Press, 1987.

Woods, Geraldine. *The Oprah Winfrey Story: Speaking Her Mind.* Minneapolis: Dillon Press, 1991.

INDEX

PICTURE CREDITS

——————— •◖◗• ———————

LOIS P. NICHOLSON holds a bachelor of science degree in elementary education and a master's degree in education from Salisbury State University. She has worked as a school librarian in both elementary and middle schools in Rock Hall, Maryland. She is the author of two other biographies for Chelsea House: *George Washington Carver* in the JUNIOR WORLD BIOGRAPHIES series and *Michael Jackson* in the BLACK AMERICANS OF ACHIEVEMENT series. In addition, she has written *Cal Ripken, Jr.: Quiet Hero* (Tidewater Publishers, 1993), and is currently writing a children's biography of Georgia O'Keeffe.

NATHAN IRVIN HUGGINS, one of America's leading scholars in the field of black studies, helped select the titles for the BLACK AMERICANS OF ACHIEVEMENT series, for which he also served as senior consulting editor. He was the W. E. B. Du Bois Professor of History and of Afro-American Studies at Harvard University and the director of the W. E. B. Du Bois Institute for Afro-American Research at Harvard. He received his doctorate from Harvard in 1962 and returned there as a professor in 1980 after teaching at Columbia University, the University of Massachusetts, Lake Forest College, and the California State University, Long Beach. He was the author of four books and dozens of articles, including *Black Odyssey: The Afro-American Ordeal in Slavery*, *The Harlem Renaissance*, and *Slave and Citizen: The Life of Frederick Douglass*, and was associated with the Children's Television Workshop, National Public Radio, the Boston Athenaeum, the Museum of Afro-American History, the Howard Thurman Educational Trust, and Upward Bound. Professor Huggins died in 1989, at the age of 62, in Cambridge, Massachusetts.